Contents

INTRO

Covid, huh! What is it good for? Absolutely nothing. Apologies to Edwin Starr. Obviously that's not true. Of course it was, and still is an awful disease, but without it this book, along with many others, would not exist. Through the medium of social media and Zoom in particular, the world of poetry opened up. People we would have never known about would have remained locked away in their own local scene, generally speaking. The poetry village became a town, growing into a city, expanding into a continent where borders don't exist and opportunities are plentiful.

 Back in August of 2020, I decided I would jump on the Zoom show bandwagon and start my own open mic. Looking for a name, I decided on utilising the title of an old poem of mine about televangelists; Like A Blot From The Blue.

During the latter months of 2020, I decided to branch out into making poetry films, with the help of my now growing group of friends from the world of spoken and written word. Then when lockdown in Scotland finally lifted for good, I produced my first live open mic. Although these aren't so regular they continue to introduce new people to the Blot family, whom we call Blotters. A few far flung friends have traveled to a Aberdeen to take part, and when I say far flung I mean it. Australia and Bradford . You don't get further than that. Well, you do, but nobody from New Zealand has ever appeared on Blot.

Then last year I put on the first spoken word festival in my village. My hard to get to village of New Pitsligo.

Little did I know that three years from the first show, Blot would have attracted so many participants from all over the globe. Literally. People from five continents have taken part in my events, something I will always be proud of, even if they have come along only once.

To help celebrate the third anniversary of Like A Blot From The Blue, I decided the best way to thank everyone was to publish this book. A poem from the world of poets to the world of poets. I can only but thank you all for always being willing to join in my projects.

May words never fail you.

This book is dedicated to Blotters everywhere.

BLOTTERS'

JOTTERS

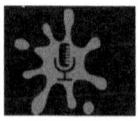

Published by Like A Blot From The Blue

New Pitsligo, Scotland 2023. ©

BUYING A BODY (£79.99)

Unlikely as it sounds it is true I swear
You can purchase a body
Without seeking assistance
From a modern iteration of Burke & Hare

On a recent visit to M&S
I discovered this
You really can
Buy a body for eighty pounds or less

A magic garment which lifts and separates those two mates
Which used to be pert breasts
So they won't be mistaken for scatter cushions
Or footrests

Tense elastic will grab your bum cheeks in a sling
To reduce their size if that's your thing
It can move your butt around if that's your desire
A little bit lower, a whole lot higher

I cannot explain how I found myself there
Wandering like an innocent amongst underwear
Like Father Ted's priests-lost-in-lingerie-department nightmare
I can only confirm this is what happened, that I swear
Peter A. Airdrie, Scotland

IN THE FOREST BEHIND THE CITY.

You, running through the forest
six years old, your
mother's windpipe tight and burning
trying to breathe
your child-legs moving forward

disconnected from the other world
your family fast and silent
rushing into the trees, leaving
the weak and captured to the beasts,
pushing through soft mountain air
no one could take in
for the gasping,
for the frantic fluttering of lungs.

Saving these children
means leaving their grandmother
to be swallowed by
bullets and a lake,
means barricading the brain
against the sight of him
taken to bleed into the veins
of eight thousand other dying fathers and sons
by someone else's fathers and sons
someone who didn't raise them
for murder
who didn't stop them
from murdering --
who couldn't or wouldn't --

means a choice every night ever after
between the terror of nightmares
and the debilitating dark nothingness

means years from then
in our America

people will say, *Oh!*
The war trouble in Bosnia
like they say, *Oh!*
the war trouble in Syria
like they say, *Oh!*
the cartel murders in Mexico
like they say, *Oh!*
the kidnappings in Nigeria

will see there on your forehead
that faint writing:

> mother lost husband, father
> died in genocide, grandmother
> died in genocide.
> Lived in temporary shelter
> during war, was
> a teenager just after.

will see you here in your
beautiful black dress, your soft eyes,
and see you here, a scholar now,
successful in the world of words and laws,
laughing at the funny ways
our kitchen switches work
while you stand inside
your six-year-old feet
bleeding your father's blood,
breathing air through your mother's struggling lungs
choosing every day between

that tattoo and *this* portfolio,
being seen as *that now-returned child war refugee*
or *this esteemed researcher from abroad*
that survivor and *this published writer*
that Bosnian and *this human being.*

What is the answer? I guess
we can never be whole
without touching the jagged cracks, cutting
through our skin a little,
without counting the negative space
where the pieces are missing
as part of the world itself

An answer? I guess there isn't one.
Let's just sit here together
in silence,
not understanding the human part of
the world beneath logic and historical explanation
until we laugh at kitchen switches
and malfunctioning coffee pots
and the necessity of vegetables and
the sweetness of fruit
and carpets stained by dogs with
lipstick between their toes
and the weird things you'll see in hardware stores
and supermarkets

until the hour
when we all go alone to choose

between remembering and forgetting
between the peaceful blankness of a night
without dreams
and the untenable blankness of a life
without the truth.

In the forest behind the city
is the slight hollow of the moss
that grows over the dirt
where you fell before your mother
lifted you without stopping
and pulled you toward
that temporary refuge.
  Nina Adel. Nashville, Tennessee USA

BUILT

Riddle me this:

WHICH IS WORSE?
        Being depicted in
            History lessons
                As villains
OR
        Being erased from
            History lessons
                Completely?
WHICH?
        Your grade schools
            Are veering

In that direction.
It's the 2nd stage following
The gradual erasing
Of Blacks from reality
By cop,
By bigot,
By our own hands,

WE ARE BEING ERASED.
Now we're not
Allowed to keep records
Or teach our young on them!

NOT IN YOUR CLASSROOMS.
By statewide,
Countywide bans,
By firing teachers who dare to share,
OUR HISTORY STAYS BURIED.
The grasp of truth
About this land's beginnings
Sacrificed
FOR YOUR CHILDREN'S COMFORT.
Lest we forget,
By force AND
Force of will,
My people constructed
This country's, this state's
This city's, this town's
Infrastructure
Your people,

Prejudiced people, repeatedly
  Claim as
YOUR GREAT ACHIEVEMENTS.
As sure as
  Sunset brings
    Day to an end,
My ancestors have built
  All your blue eyes survey.
As sure as
  Descendants of the
    United Slaves to America want reparations,
My ancestors have built, All your blue eyes survey.
BLACK HANDS
Have raised your sky-scraping
Buildings from the ground on up,
Paved your roadways w/ cement & gravel,
Pieced together those strong, sturdy
Iron bridges over water, the ones
You cross on morning & evening auto commutes,
Drove buses, trains & cable cars
To send YOU to work, home &
The neighbourhood bar,
Toiled in your factories, warehouses,
Offices & power plants,
Rocked your loud crying babies to sleep,
Cleaned from front to back
The rooms of YOUR HOMES,
Laid down miles of iron track & wood,
Hammered in the spikes for
Railroads along w/ yellow hands

For the same criminally low wage,

Tended to open fields of vegetation—

Vegetables, grains, fruit, sugarcane

And yes, King Cotton—

So all of you can eat well

& wear decent clothes—

1 city in particular—

    Former home of mine—

        Was burnt to a crisp in

A war between states—

    Arose from war's ashes : Like a phoenix in the southeast

ATLANTA

Rebuilt

    W/ work

        From Black prisoners, White corporate punishment—

SLAVERY SURVIVED IN ANOTHER FORM.

Conflict like this,

    Between races,

        Between classes,

Lie @ the heart

    Of Amerikkka's & Capitalism's

        Conjoined past—

As sure as

    Wet & dry

        Are opposite feelings,

My ancestors have built

    All your blue eyes survey.

 Including your schools.

Riddle me this:

HOW LONG
Do you think
   Your laws can prevent
      Truth from reaching young ears?
HOW LONG?
The spotlight
   Is
     Switched off
On tales of Europe,
   The original 13 colonies,
     The 1st Thanksgiving dinner.

EUROCENTRISM STOPS HERE.
One-sided
   Stars & stripes Liberty
     Sugar coat from your schools
Sweetened young minds
   Enough to forget
     Their own struggles to survive here—
Riddle me this
1 last thing:
W/out our hands,
   W/out our legwork,
     W/out our labour,
HOW WILL YOUR CIVILISATION RUN?
Dee Allen Oakland California

LADIES O' SCOTLAND

Tack a bow
Tack a seat
& rest yer feet,
Fir a while now;

It is tae you
Scotsmen owe the greatest debt,
Men tend tae be mayre so myopic
Nay matter the givin' topic
Weemen are nay nearly sae inept;

The Great Scotch Lady,
Whar wid' we be wee oot
The back bone o' the nation
I proclaim thee wee this oration;
O' this I hae nae doobt."
Uillieam Màc Alisdair. Aberdeen, Scotland

A DAY@ LEVITTOWN LONG ISLAND NEW YORK IN 70's.   *1*

A winter day @ Levittown, Long Island, New York where I stay @ 70s.
The winter was chilly. With 4 ft of snow. 17 degree.
The snow cascading like icing powder dusting @ the naked trees.
I laid on the snow ground. Fluttered my hands. A snow angel appeared sending a cheery smile.
Snow covered cars lined Levittown street. Like icy lollipop.

I was expecting some guests for dinner.
I seasoned the orange duck. With fresh orange juice in the stomach. I added ginger, garlic, orange peel, cinnamon stick, 3 Tbs rice wine, 4 Tbs light soya sauce, Tbs oyster sauce. Sew it with thread. Roast orange duck at
180 Degree C, 350 Deg F 45 mins.

I put sea bass in a plate. Add 3 Tbs light soya sauce, 1 Tbs oyster sauce, 2 Tbs rice wine.
Add spring onion, shredded ginger, chopped garlic, sliced chilly.
Steam the sea bass for 15 mins.

Smiles from the guests with nod of approval for my cooking.
When you treat.your friends like king & queen. Your friends Will relish you.
Sylvia Ang. Singapore

DO YOU (REDACTED)

Do you blame yourself?
What?
Well, it's quite common in this situation for a patient to feel a kind of guilt.
What situation?
The accident.
What accident?!?!
The accident that's been haunting you from the beginning of time to now
Stalking all your movements like reaching to (REDACTED)
Chasing all of your words like asking for (REDACTED)
Mashing all of your feelings like watching (REDACTED)
Chewing all of your opinions like when you was in a conversation with
(REDACTED)
Ignoring your every plea and cry like when you was (REDACTED)
It wraps itself around your world with one goal in mind: Destruction just like how you
wished to be a (REDACTED)
Tendrils full of hatred stabbing your eyes , draining your brain of freedom just like the
time when you (REDACTED)
Claws rich and full of disgust digging within your heart, dissecting your purposes
away like cutting out the (REDACTED)
Blades coloured black like your very heart
drilling into your soul emptying it of all
Colour and life, like throwing away your (REDACTED)
Leaving you a soulless, hollow container
Being a creature of higher power known as (REDACTED)
So, I'll ask you again do you blame yourself for the accident?
Only this time you'll have found out what is was being known in earthen language as
"Existing"
wasting potential stardust on things like (FOREVER REDACTED)
Mickey Angel. Wolverhampton, England

THERE WAS A FLY

There was a little black fly that time

Refereeing the truth of my adoption

At the dining room table

We drank three bottles

Of whisky

It's been following me

All my life

Sometimes it has friends

Sometimes alone in the winter

Watching the snowflakes caresses

The empty pavement

We rowed that night

You called me a bastard

Which technically is true

With your broken finger pointing

Like a dervishes knife

I asked you for a fight outside, the only time

Only real Father of mine.

I thought the fly an omen

You said it was a living being

You understood the universe

Told me not to crush insects

Now your no longer a living being

But the fly is still here sometimes

A gentle reminder of your reverence

Of nature

And snowflakes still fall

As they wind their lonely path

Around my house

And I sometimes look for footsteps

Michael Arthur. Aberdeen, Scotland

PARISH COUNCIL

sultry centrist,
simping, prostrate
to miss the mark
of mawed maxims
'bout 'early birds' -

*"what's for you
won't run by you"*,
mori-gramps said;
but, a small town talks

and ad-lib words oft'

dib that stoic, heroic,
strong but silent
churn. all such
stolid masc a myth
best unearthed.
Barney Ashton-Bullock. London England

THAT HAIR

I finally got that hair.
I was actually able to pluck it.
You know the one -
that single, solitary hair
growing on the left side of my face
right in the middle of the cheek?
How did it get there? Why is it growing all alone?
What does it all mean?
More importantly.. WHY ME??
I finally got that hair
after plucking all the peach fuzz
surrounding and mounting the rest of my skin
and, ouch!.. pulling peach fuzz hurts!
sometimes my tweezer gets itself around that hair,
but the thrust of the pull isn't enough to GET.. IT.. OUT.
but today was different.
I couldn't believe it!
I finally got that hair
and it took only 10 tries.
I think that alone deserves a medal,
if not bandaids to cover all the other gauges in my skin now.
But I finally got that hair!
You know the one -
that elusive, slippery hair
growing all by its' lonesome
which I hadn't been able to pluck!
do you think it gets lonely living there so isolated?
or, does it get its' jollies knowing it's driving me crazy.

I vote for the latter.
oh, that hair!!
C S Badin. Georgia, USA
THE HARBOURS WE SAIL TO.   *2*

"...It's the dream we carry in secret
that something miraculous will happen,
that one morning we will glide into
some little harbour we didn't know was there."
"Olav H. Hauge (1966)
Translated by Scottish poet Robin Fulton
Rq

How many harbours has my nation seen?

Some close, familiar, that we knew all the entries of
Some unexpectedly similar
despite being so far away

Most turned - thankfully - very friendly
We knew about some
Or sailed to unknown shores

The lands of mystical beasts
Great whales
Seductive sirens
Lands that our imagination has created
Rather than being true to themselves
And definitely the majority of us
Has never dreamt
Of seeing them live.

We keep dreaming
Both in secret and daringly open
To the whole world
Surprising our neighbours
Surprising ourselves

The dreams are being broken
Stolen
Just to be created again

We kept getting up
No matter how many times
our dreams were betrayed
Each generation lost the best people
To be turned into national heroes
And create motivation for new times.

We don't believe in miracles
Not the given ones
For we know that the only lasting ones
Are the miracles we create by ourselves.
Leysa Bakun. Ukraine/Norway

AN ODE TO SMUDGE

On a painting or in a book,
A smudge must be removed,
A stain that is a source of pain,
An unplanned mark that remains
Creating consternation.
A weed is a plant growing
In a space where it is unwanted.
What of those on the Isle of Misfit toys?
What of the lost girls and boys?

So, a toast to Bob Ross:
A smudge is not a mistake but a happy accident.
Take a look, and another, a third or a fourth.
Discover possibilities that now exist, serendipity!
When you next see a smudge, give it a hug
Don't hold a grudge and don't rub it out.
Kemlyn Tan Bappe, Phoenix, Arizona., USA.

UNTITLED

If I told you all that happened

The words and the way that they were said

If I told you how he touched me

How his breath felt on my neck

If I told you how it made me feel

The thoughts inside my head

The way it still affects me

The choices that I made

If I told you how I froze, was silent

Just stood there in a haze

Would you blame me like I blamed myself

Would your picture of me change

If you knew you'd want to fix it

Take away the pain

Make it like it never happened

Go back and start again

But then we'd both be sad

Its part of who I am

So I say nothing, to protect you

Because if I told you, you'd go mad

Rachel Beedie. Aberdeen, Scotland.

STAYCATION

Man, I hate Staycation!
More than lurking in cold
Bus stations!
Much more, the current
Holiday, invocation -
I fucking hate that word –
Staycation!

No, its not the going away,
I love the occasional holiday
The trips to the North West Highlands and
Grunar Bay, with its pure white sands.
Driving down the seventy-four
I love the yearly pilgrimage to Somerset
The beautiful light of their sunset
That's when I quite like our United nation
But, fuck me, how much I hate Staycation!

It comes from the same stable as Brunch!
Just bloody decide, is it breakfast or lunch?
And please don't tell me to chillax
And piss off asking, "..if I fill to the max?"
I love the thought of great recreation
But fuck me , how much I hate, Staycation!

I miss writing postcards and
Piss smelling phone boxes
Muddy walking boots and hand knitted sockses
Cold chips, mixed with green mushy peas
Holidays at home, are all filled with these
And I've been to the States, on many vacations
But fuck me, how much I hate Staycation!

Staycation, staycation – the curse of our nation
Take a break. A day off. Holiday participation
In caravans, motorhomes, or down by the sea

A greasy cooked breakfast in an old B+B

Whatever you do for your respite sensation.
Enjoy, girl or boy with Pug or Dalmatian
Just please, please don't go on a
Fucking
Staycation

Chris Begg, Aberdeen, Scotland

VULNERABILITY :THE UNDOING OF FALSE LOVE

I took that ring off

No, not out of dread or something you said there simply was no way ahead and the light?
Well the light inside had died and yet here I am fully alive to the wonders of what lies ahead

Life is a mystery and I could not hide behind a ring that lied of a relationship
I brushed aside all the questions and entered the rhythm of new things as the life
I lived has died
It wasn't that I sought new things

I didn't need to hide behind a ring acting as cover, as if there was another
I was enough alone
No need to be owned

Too much was at stake. My integrity and for the sake of my own voice I sail on the
course of mystery. I am enough and free and it's best if you see me as I really
am without a ring to give me cover or to hide behind

I am not blind and can receive this grace in new ways - it is our fate
Throughout my life I've known the course of love is unending
and I can wait. I can wait.
Thérèse M. Craine Bertsch. Saville. NY, USA.

CAREFREE

On the lake this morning
The water was still

Sleeping in its bed
Dreaming in the wind

Swans passed by
In a straight line
Could it be a mother
Small ones following

So close
Then gone
Just a glimpse
A moment of joy

Observations
A time without worries
Nature knows
What is right
Antje Bothin, Hamilton, Scotland

I AM GRATEFUL FOR LIFE

I am grateful for this vessel that has allowed me to Travel millions of life times, hours, and selves through Travel of astral amounts that can never be told

For being one that breaks the mold

I am grateful for my body's decay

The wear and tear of everyday

I am grateful for my crackly ankle that still carries me

It speaks of all the steps that has brought me to thee

I am grateful for the sun in my window waking me

And a view of the sky so breathtakingly

I am grateful for the knowledge of knowing why

I am grateful for the release of tears I cry

I am grateful for the abundance coming to me

Even all of the things I cant yet see

I am grateful for friends and family

I am grateful for being who and what I am

Way-showing others to far away land

I am grateful for things I haven't yet received

I am grateful for opportunities to sit by the sea

All of these things to be grateful for

And that today my feet hit the floor

Making the bed

And having coffee too

And most of all I am grateful for you

Danelle Boyles. United States

THE PENUMBRA

Ive been picking up the pieces of a heart I didn't break.

And romanticising colours

On a backdrop of mistakes.

We conjured songs between us, In a language no one knew. Roots were tangled underneath A land where nothing grew.

I can sometimes feel you dreaming,

On a mountain never scaled,

As you serenade the fire

With no-one there to hear our tale.

But love, there are no whimpers,

That could transcend what was true.

And somewhere deep within those flames, My colours bleed for you.

Kelly Buchan. St Combs, Scotland

UNCONSCIOUS MIND

I try and stay conscious to find my unconscious mind

As I close my eyes for the darkness, in this vastness of blackened out skies.

I'm conscious to block out any sound, that comfortably surrounds me

and focus, intently, on gently easing my way into my unconscious memory

I try and relax while my lungs slowly deflate

through the calmness of night, my mind is alert in search of that, higher state.

I'm sure I see patterns and silhouettes and then shapes

as I try and urge my soul from my body, to consciously find my unconscious state.

My eyes are closed but I think I can consciously see.

Although not much makes sense, at the moment. I try and set my mind free.

I'm hoping to find something clear that I see A vision that isn't just only a dream.

Al Buchanan. New Pitsligo, Scotland

A HUNDRED YEARS AFTER WILFRED OWEN'S ' FUTILITY'
FOR THE STATUS IN BIRKENHEAD

Put the soldier's statue,
On a corner, opposite the square.
Named like the poem, 'Futility'
Sits near the cenotaph that keeps score,
Of those who were lost in battles won.
All the statue can do today is warn:
War games aren't played for fun.

Shake hands politicians,
For honouring the heroes who die.
Their blood turns black your profit-margins
When you sell arms for the M.O.D.
Is it for this war-machine we mourn
Their blown arms, their left legs, their right minds,
And fake poppies get worn?
Caroline Burrows. Bristol, England
This poem was first published in The Wilfred Owen Journal Volume 2 2020.
and then online by the Rainbow Poems: Remembrance Edition 2020

THE LOST ART OF LIGHTING A POEM

Gather kindling and if you are in a hurry, douse it
with inflammable or flammable ideas
(either will work they are the same)
Take two sticks and rub them furiously together

(you can also do this in good temper).

Light your poem and stand well back
Don't lose an eye like Odin for the sake of your art.
Don't let it become an inferno it's been done.
Don't leave your poem unattended as it may attract
magpie poets or worse Prometheus .
Remember to put your poem, once cool, out
into the worlds, this can be into the virtual world or the real one.
(It doesn't matter they are the same)
Vagabond poets may (or may not) gather at the site
of your conflagration (this is what you'll call it to the press) .
Remember, no two poems should be the same,
unless you borrowed your ideas, sticks,
and kindling from another fire starter.
If you like you could rake through the ashes
of your poetry pit to find something worth keeping.
This exercise can be repeated every day
until people are so sick of the scorched earth
you leave behind that they try to have you arrested.

Tell the poetry police when they arrive
your fires are metaphorical, this should prevent legal action.
Try not to mention similes, as it's an offence these days
and anyway we all know what similes are like.
We've all seen them in the lines of redundant fire starters
who sit in shadow, their forgotten faces turned to profile
waiting to become fashionable in vain.
Jack Caradoc, Dunfermline, Fife, Scotland.

HANDS

The outstretched hand, a sign of a friend
an elderly person, a hand to lend.
A warm handshake, so firm, so strong,
reassuring to feel we belong.

Hands cradling the babe to feel secure
Rocking to and fro - a love so pure.
The touch of the nurse so full of grace

to ease the pain on a troubled face.

Lover's caress, wiping away tears,
to bring back joy, allay all fears.
A pat on the back when things go right,
a clenched fist, symbol of a fight.

The artist creating works of art,
the canvas complete uplifts the heart.
The pianist tinkling his ivory keys,
melodies tunefully set to please.

The chef creating food with flair,
families together, memories share.
Old hands - wrinkles of lives so full,
time spent gardening or working with tools.

Hands say more than we'll ever know,
our gestures, feelings, our nature's on show.
Let them be comforting, loving, sharing,
Let them demonstrate peace and caring.
Elizabeth A Carey, Dalry, North Ayrshire.Scotland.
This piece was featured in INKLINGS published by Ravenshoe Writers in
Queensland Australia in 2018 under the title Hand Gestures.

CHAOS AND MIDNIGHT

Somewhere between chaos and midnight
I can love you there
my evening terrors never stop
Always with me everywhere
Even when a new level is unlocked

My subconscious has many triggers
these anxieties make it hard for me
try so much to trust
with all that I have
hope it's even enough

Can you love the pieces

that are left of me
the shards I melted back together
with roots that I am trying to plant

Knowing now that I can water myself
enough to make me grow
turning and facing the sun
glowing bright
my future seems to be in sight

Dreamt of being free
now it has really come to be
however my nightmares keep going
even when feelings continue free flowing

Hoping and waiting
Dancing under the pale moonlight
somewhere between
chaos and midnight…
 Black Widow
Gina Carrillo. Franklin, TN USA

HUG

My mother's heart was a lake,

its frozen surface cracked,

when I was young, with

insults hurled her way,

and I hurled many, wounding

like rocks, till her cool glaze

became a starburst of splintered love.

Even her delight in daffodils,

withered, since the bunch of yellow bells

she gave me on my 15th birthday,

whose whole heads I bit off, mad at her

for some imagined slight and in an
acid spritz of blame, spat her way,

at which my mother, murmuring to herself,
sure the poor girl's tired,
patted my arm, our only
physical exchange,
for we never hugged.

Having learnt, years later,
how an infant monkey
languishes if deprived
of its mother's touch,
I subjected her
to a lingering clinch.

Not just a brief *ooh-la-la* peck
on either cheek, stay
two feet away
from-one-another sort of hug,
but a bellytobelly chesttochest
squeeze, palming up and down her back
as though grooming the silk-eyed Persian
hunkered on the couch, glaring,
and on a normal day, the only flesh
my mother or myself would handle.

And when she tried to edge away,
I fastened my grip like
now I've got you ma, you're

going nowhere. The way,

when small, I ached for her

to hold me, limpet tight
Veronica Castle. West Sussex. England

WHERE THE BIRDS DON'T FLY

The places where buildings crumble like sandcastles.
The sky coloured ashen
with explosive residue.
Where the sacrificial lambs wage power's battles.
The borders flooded by the advancing tides,
rushing towards safer sands,
propelled by a hostile surge.
Taking only their frantically bagged lives.
The homes where sirens turn the blood cold.
The blasts, increasingly louder.
Young fearfully, questioning eyes
find no answers. Strategic chaos takes hold.
In the ruins where the tears run dry.
Reclaim the dead from the debris.
Only the dead are free.
Without a song where the birds don't fly.
Nayma Chamchoun. London, England
Originally Published in, COVID: THE WORDY WILDS OF A MIND UNDER
LOCKDOWN October 2022 by Mica Press

A LETTER IN MY POCKET

The world is full of rainbows and waterfalls,

That sparkle in the sun.

Shimmering like happy, hazy memories,

And powerful promises of what's yet to come.

The world is blessed with blossoming branches,

And lined with mighty Rowan.

Basalt 'tites, and icy 'mites,

That fill each lava cavern.

So stay awake, please,

Just a little longer, Nan.

I've got a letter in my pocket,

From your great grandson.

The world is full of snow-covered clifftops,

Of whale-song from frozen fjords.

And black beaches, hemmed with birch trees,

Where in the summer, nest puffin birds.

The world is capped with majestic glaciers,

That trundle, at their own pace.

Taking in the beauty of their surroundings,

In no mad rush, to fill their face.

So stay awake, please,

Just a little longer, Nan.

I've got a letter in my pocket,

From your great grandson.

The world is full of powerful geysers,

Sat upon a hill.

Leaving vast craters in their wakes,

Raining down with brimstone, til all is still.

The world is at war;

Always has been, always will be.

No right, nor wrong, just political pacts,

Power, profit, and policy.

So stay awake, please,

Just a little longer, Nan.

I've got a letter in my pocket,

From your great grandson.

From the Viking raiders of Iceland;

Who torched the Irish monks.

To Cromwell's New Model Army;

Who torched the Irish monks.

Two great wars, an eternal slave trade,

And the plight of Palestine.

European imperialism, dollar diplomacy,

And communism, at its most extreme.

So stay awake, please,

Just a little longer, Nan.

I've got a letter in my pocket,

From your great grandson.

The world is full of potential,

Of hope; where blasts and bombs rescind.

Where Putin's power is powerless,

And Boris's bluster, just echoes in the wind.

Where doves fly over mountain tops,

And seagulls circle overhead.

Where peace is power, and justice reigns.

And the tanks are put to bed.

So stay awake, please,

Just a little longer, Nan.

I've got a letter in my pocket,

From your great grandson.

The youth of today, frighten their elders,

Because they recycle, and protest, and care.

They don't smack their kids; they don't vote Tory.

They listen, and learn, and care.

The world is full of rainbows and waterfalls,

That sparkle in the sun.

Shimmering like hazy, happy memories,

And powerful promises of what's yet to come.

So stay awake, please,

Just a little longer, Nan.

I've got a letter in my pocket,

From your great grandson.

Liam Christopher West Midlands, UK

MAMBO URBANO

Mambo is

a street beat,

the rat-tat-tat rain

on a tin roof shack,

the swoosh of a wave,

monsoon wind

through wispy willows,

a Gulf Coast shore line...

Mambo is

the boom-boom-boom

Bembe beating drum call,

a Dixieland cornet,

Congo Square Black Creole

Mardi Gras Indians,

second line dancing,

the echo of a jungle call

and answer...

Mambo is

Octaroon Jonconnu Trenchtown

redemption songs,

the clackety-clack chink-a-chink

Sao Paolo cable car creeping

steep Samba hills,

Carnaval streets teeming

ten thousand bodies bouncing and

the bum-bum-bum badum-bum

Bossa beat and bustle of a

Rio night bohemian cafe

thick Bahia twilight mystery

en la madrugada...

Mambo is

La Bodeguita del Media Havana moon,

dockside Rumba ritmo,

bawdy bard Decima duels,

calling and answering,

boasting and bantering,

beating

from El Alhambra

from Santiago de Cuba,

Oriente Son and sea meet

montuno Yoruba beat,

cool street and

jungle heat

in the pulse

of Mambo...

Mambo is

calloused hands

on smooth skin djembe,

worn sticks striking

hollow logs of history,

rant-a-tang cowbells,

a hundred pan drummers

Trini Fete Jump up! Jump up!

Tuve morning come

Candomble Espirite Brasile,

Pocomania downtown

sidewalk Santeros,

tenement saints,

like drumming in the walls

like drumming in the halls

of Harlem and Queens

Port au Prince and New Orleans,

like saxophone sounding

sweet home Southside Chicago,

A Capella singing on

a South Philly stoop,

talking drum whispering,

a whoop, a whoop,

reed flute whistling

crisp Andean heights,

the ghost of a poet

outside City Lights,

a Salvadoran revolucionista

whose song is conviction,

Jose Marti in Nueva York,

his Guajira a longing,

Cardenal en Nicaragua,

his poem revelation,

his sermon revolution...

Mambo is

like rivers that flow

from mountain streams,

restlessly downward

through towering redwoods,

bold Balboa,

past Buddha Bodhi tree

and blackberry bushes,

past morning doves cooing

in marshland bulrushes,

like the catch-a-chatch chop of

a cane cutter's clave...

Mambo is

the river that flows

through empty hamlets and

half sleeping towns,

silently slipping through

sanitized suburbs

of manicured lawns,

past cold granite court houses

in old town squares,

past playgrounds

the rhythm of innocent laughter,

past parking lot dances

of tires and glass and plastic and metal,

past white-washed warehouse echoes

the songs of fork lift whine

and diesel truck rumble,

through factory gates

that swing like pendulums

under Golgotha smokestacks,

through rust iron rail yards,

under long swaying bridges,

through smoldering barrio

simmering tropic hood,

under 'L tracks and trains

through forests towering

steel and glass...

Mambo is

just down the street,

the pulse and the beat,

tap-tapping feet,

the funky and sweet,

Azucar! Sabroso!

and Roque singing of

La Augusta Dame de la Clase Media,

of Buses Urbanos,

and Pablo singing

of poems that rise

from rushing waters,

Papa Hemingway singing

an old man and the sea,

Machito singing

all night Mambo Cubano,

La Señora Celia singing

life as a carnival,

Willie Colon

singing sizzling salsa,

even Allen singing

his saintly locomotive sunflower

singing sutras of midnight jazz,

of beatitudes and bohos,

of painters and prophets,

poesia and pain,

of black cat Blues

and hot steam asphalt,

of August rains

and mountain streams,

of cities

of streets

of rhythm

of dance

of taxicab horns

of streetcar rattles

of power line hums

of claves

of maracas

of guiro

of congas

of vozes

of Rumba

of Guaguanco

of Bomba

of Changui

of Son

of Mambo

of Mambo

of Mambo Urbano

Philip Christopher, Indianapolis, Indiana, USA

1st Printing The Caribbean Writer, Vol 19 (2005)

AN HONEST PROPOSAL

My dear, my love, please accept my hand in marriage.
There's nothing more romantic I can think of.
Just think of it.

Think of the lovely life we'll share.
Think of the rapturous wedding we'll hold.
Think of the passionate honeymoon.
Think of the limitless lovemaking.
Think of the joy of stepping into our first house.
Think of the tears we'll shed when our first child is born.
Think of the pride we'll feel watching our child grow up.
Think of the slightly fewer tears we'll shed when our second child is born.
Think of the stretch marks you'll have.
Just think of it.

Think of the years of family dinners spent together.
Think of the birthday parties and Xmas mornings.
Think of the endless school hockey games and plays.
Think of the countless sibling fights we'll break up.
Think of the disappointing report cards.
Think of the minimal amount of tears we'll shed when our third child is born.
Think of the neglect our middle child'll suffer.
Think of the times our middle child'll act out because of our neglect.
Think of the moment the cop'll tell us our middle child has been arrested for vandalism.
Just think of it.

Think of the dull daily routine into which our lives'll plummet.

Think of the day we'll stop going out without the children.
Think of the evenings sitting in front of the TV and never speaking to each other.
Think of the passive-aggressive verbal jabs we'll poke at each other.
Think of the moment we'll forget what we saw in each other in the first place.
Think of the screaming arguments our children'll overhear when they're in bed.
Think of the slamming doors and hurled plates.
Think of the silent treatments and insincere apologies.
Think of the therapy bills our children'll pay.
Just think of it.

Think of the night I'll catch you receiving cunnilingus from my brother's weightlifting trainer.
Think of the condescending tone you'll adopt to mock my sexual inadequacy.
Think of the tiny basement apartment into which I'll move.
Think of the vicious, exhausting court battle we'll prolong for months.
Think of the enormous legal bills and time wasted.
Think of the way we'll make our children choose which of us they love more.
Think of the friends we'll lose and the gossip they'll share.
Think of the size my belly'll grow as I just stop caring.
Think of the botched plastic surgery that'll symbolize your desperate drive to stay young.
Just think of it.
Think of the thousands of lonely nights of TV dinners and masturbation.
Think of the chronic online stalking of old high-school crushes.
Think of the ugl—

Oh, you're leaving?
I suppose you need more time to think.

I'll be waiting here, with this beautiful tungsten wedding ring.

A life together. Just think of it.
Jeff Cottrill. Toronto Canada.

GAMBLING

Scabby discarded and broken
left sitting offset on the pavement
its shine as cracked and broken
as it's weary bling coloured dots

Rolled a six again,
ye ken yer doon on yer luck
when ye look oan and curse...

As the snake says 'when?'

Then moves tae the side to let ye sidle past
tae the ladder awaiting yer descent
Wi hand grips that fit ye
like gloves new knitted that day

Ye'd hae argued the toss
bit whits the point
When you've lost at cards
And yer horse's long bolted

So doon the ladder ye slide
doon and doon till yer
back whaur ye started
oan rung number one

and no a fuckin ladder in sight.

Sometimes looking doon
gies ye a start oan something
that's oan the up

If only ye can grasp that first rung .
Janet Crawford. Falkirk, Scotland
published in Razur Cuts 8 & Razur Cuts Finest Cuts -Best of the first five years-
anthology .

ROTATION

Vildledt i omfavnelsen
svinger tanker i ordlyd
rundt om bevægelsen
mod et fælles sted, hvis
begrundelse ligger i
bølgerne, men ses som
vægge, som sætter
grænse for de kastede

flag. Havet imponerer
sjældent, mens det
tabte samles op igen.

Rotation
Deluded in the embrace,
thoughts in words oscillate
around the movement
towards a common place,
whose justification lies in
the waves, but can be seen
as walls, that
limit the thrown
flags. The sea rarely
impresses, while the
lost is picked up again.
Poul Lynggaard Damgaard. Denmark
" Boks sepia", 2013

FREE OUT FROM THE IRON CAGE HONOURING MY MIND

To all writers in prison having a voice
Winter - without clothes, only rug pyjamas in winter
winter, winter, winter with iron teeth
the teeth are biting from my flesh
once a day a watery coffee
without shadowy-traces of coffee beans
and loneliness, deep muddy loneliness
but I fly in my mind ...mind
I'm feeling in my brain the love
love of my ally. above the sky what
I'm seeing in a corner of the
small high window
the voice of my lover
abstract voice and neutered voice
touching my face, my skin, my heart.
 'remember only that I was innocent
and just like you, mortal on that day,
I, too, had had a face marked
by rage, pity, and joy
quite simply, a human face"
I'm carrying on my prisoner wings

faiths, desires, dreams...
of all earth's inmates ....even
even if I will die, I will be tortured
I will be oppressed for my voice
for my thoughts, for my choice
because I fly--
I fly with my power, I fly with my suffering
and my smile for this wonderful world
yes. my suffering, my death, my humiliation
will talk, talk, talk about our captive world!
'we need people to speak
loudly against injustice...'
Spring - is coming, and birds
are singing in the prison's courtyard
males and females, beautiful birds
dancing around each other with flowers
flowers in their coloured beaks.
smoothly I'm caressing one of the flowers
fallen down and keeping it to my breast
for later, for the next day, and...
for tomorrow, and tomorrow, and the tomorrow of my life
in my cell barrack with iron bar...
Punished - in this amazing spring in the sky
and on the earth....flowers are not allowed around!
prisoners, prisoners, prisoners, punished, punished, punished...
but my mind is blooming -- flowers and birds, green
leaves and coloured pools, mountains, and flowing rivers
my mind is a garden, a forest, a tree jungle, and a peaceful beach
springing out from my torture, humiliation, and suffering
my wounds, especially soul wounds,
draw the endless heavenly worlds
through ornamentation of words.
summer - is coming, yes, summer, summer
lights and the hot-yellow sun kissing my forehead
insects flying with their songs between the heights of clouds
and fresh green on the soil
But ---
I am closed in this iron coffin!
crying...never again I will kiss the lover I love
never again I will walk on the streets
never, never, being closed in this iron coffin
I will embrace my kids....kids
summer, my past beautiful summer,

please, please, let your fingers to touch my future
sister-summer...maybe in my mind, maybe...
But death! Never I will kiss my lover under
free bright summery sky...summery sky!
autumn -- my thoughts...we...we are lost in this hollow
of the dying. my thoughts -- St. Augustin says God has
reason for torture, for persecution, in our life for dark clouds
as a result of Adam who acted with 'free will" eating an apple -
my thoughts, my thoughts in autumn
Am I a sinner because a man had eaten a fruit?
my thoughts, my thoughts in autumn
' tell me, what is the bigger sin - a man eating an apple
or punishing an entire humanity with torture because
a man ate an apple? '
I am in an iron cage, I am in an iron coffin, I am in a camp-prison
barrack with teeth, iron teeth that are biting from my flesh
from my blood, throwing me into death
Am I the modern Adam? No, No, No...
I am free of his umbilical cord.
autumn...rain in my mind scratching the barrack's walls
of my iron camp, of my iron prison
' the death note is sounded,
the beasts hunted down
let me speak to you..'
I am free, flying through my mind, my voice, my thought, my desire
my voice name is Benjamin Fondane
my powerful thought is Nawal El Saadawi
my wonderful desire is Ahmet Altan
this voice, this thought, this desire was metamorphosed
from the marrow of writing, of words.
I am a writer! out from the iron cage.
my soul is free honouring my eagle warmth...honouring my mind
my mind. I am free, out of the iron cage.
Lucia Daramus. Stroud, England

BENEATH THE VERY SAME SKY

In a ritual of healing for his tribe
before the sun begins to set, the Navajo artist
will rub out all traces of his sun kissed work
pushing every grain of sand
back into the canvas of the desert

readied for sunrise; for the sand art to follow

poets have so much to learn from this
how so very hard it it is … for them, then
to feed last night's magnum opus into a shredder
to lean all the way on the backspace key
or use a thick sharpie to score out every stanza
to consign sheafs of foolscap to the fire

the Navajo sand artist gazes up at star constellations
whilst the poet ponders that oxymoron: final draft
Neil Daswani. Singapore

THE CYCLE

 Take a puff and then pause

What the fuck is a god

With all the worlds evils ending up on top

Surely that is a Flaw

Divine creation wouldn't come to

You'll argue that we're human but that's nature bearing no fruit

Mind is vacant and have no clue

future seedlings will all go through

Dusty lands and empty vocals

No choirs signing the chorus

All the voices have gone hoarse

corpses lining the floors

No escape from the new norm

Always want what came before us

Living the hard trip

We are starving

Not just artists, it's bipartisan

Never getting resolved %

It's time we flip the board

Don our shields and grab our swords

Hack and slash as we rage war

Bruce Alexander Davidson. Aberdeen, Scotland

THREE STRAYS FACE THE CAMERA

In line for his snack the black and white stray squats next to a concrete dog squeezed into

a lion's knee propped by a flowerpot.

Inert, the cat completes the triptych, poised underneath the yew, three backs to the fence.

The lion sniffs inches above his prey,

cavities for teeth, jaws a silent roar.

Bought on Dad's whim to rule in Mum's garden

he took root where the rotten elm was felled, spent years dressing the raw stump with both paws.

The dog, lop-sided, blank- eyed, a childhood friend in Essex, stood firm on home ground. Here, he's lost edge, lacks balance, needs help. We hoard the exiles when we break up homes, welcome them to the shelter of the yew.

Picture these misfits, pets caught in a flash, posed side by side, dark art like the fable, flesh stilled into artefact, turned to stone. The black and white stray waits for his snack, alert, alone. Snap and the moment's gone

Christine Dickinson. Spalding, England.

HE DIDN'T BITE

He was tame if truth be told – a curtain-twitching
kind of fool-hearted guard dog, making studies of how
others waded through the humdrum. He was sturdy
in routine, if not stature – his nose in the paper after
the Six O'clock news, on the far edge of the sofa every
night, inside-out sweaters on Saturdays & passing round
the basket in chapels on Sundays – altar boy breeding

still beaten into his being like the scars he wore on his
shoulders of all the things he could no longer put down.

From afar, you could see how fear had opened itself up
within his frame like a cushion forced to house too much
foam & the stitch strains from the stuffing. He was tame,
of course, but at the time, I was so cautious of his bite.
Damien D Donnely. Dublin, Ireland.

TIMING

The Doctor is treating me.
(ms. kateřina vonná, surgery number 31, pneumology)
She is a tall beautiful blonde young lady.
(ms. jarmila brazdilová krásná, surgery number 57, internal medicine)
She doesn't' say anything,
(mr. konrad wegener, surgery number 118, ophthalmology)
just keeps writing something.
(ms. zuzana dolejší, surgery number 12, orthopaedics)
If I wasn't ill,
(mr. oldřich pšenica, surgery number 40, cardiology)
she might become my girlfriend.
(ms. alice skovroňská, surgery number 26, otorhinolaryngology)
And what she is writing now,
(mr. anton schneider, surgery number 5, neurology)
could be
(ms. beata řehoříková, surgery number 49, oncology)
love letters to me.
mr. jaroslav černohorský, surgery number 63, dermatology)
However, for now it is probably
just my diagnosis.
(ms. anne-marie linhart, surgery number 104, gastroenterology)
Maybe when I recover ...
(mr. radek wittman, surgery number 122, urology)

(recorded by nurse on duty jani)

The nurse is taking my blood pressure and pulse.
(ms. ingrid weinberger, room number 17, department of neurology)

She is a tall beautiful blonde young lady.
(ms. tereza nováková, room number 8, accident and emergency)
She doesn't speak loud,
(mr. pavel vajda, room number 32, comfort single room, department of dermatology)
just whispering something.
(ms. olenka pavlíčková, room number 87, department of ophthalmology)
If I wasn't paralysed,
(ms. anja hanna mizumska, room number 40, intensive care unity)
she might become my wife.
(ms. aloisia kovářová, room number 118, internal medicine)
And her whispering could be romantic love messages for me.
(mr. pavel vajda, room number 61, department of hematology and blood transfusion)
However, for now, they are probably
(mr. jános király, main room, long-term care department)
only the results of my pressure and pulse measurement
(ms. judit antal, room number 55, comfort double room, department of diabetology)
Maybe when I will be able to move again ...
 (recorded by sister on duty lucka, nurse care coordinator)
The embalmer is washing and embalming
(mortuary chamber A
my stiff and cold body.
procházková alena, locker no. 27, laryngeal cancer)
She is a tall beautiful blonde lady.
(kozlovská kateřina, locker no. 108, AIDS)
She doesn't say, doesn't write, doesn't whisper anything,
(šavrdová lucie, locker no. 62, diabetes)
she is just looking again and again
(rajka klement, locker no. 75, heart attack)
at the watch in the wall.
(blanenský petr, locker no. 32, alcoholic coma)
If I wasn't dead
(mortuary chamber B
she could become my love
nová lavinie, locker no. 44, tuberculosis)
and she would keep looking at that clock because
(winterberger hannelore, locker no. 137, kidney failure)
she would be looking forward to meet me as soon as possible.
(zograffi tadeáš, locker no. 91, multiple sclerosis)
But now it is probably because .
(bílá grazziela, locker no. 114, natural death)
she is looking forward to the end of the working day
(konvalinková tereza, locker no. 109, natural death)
and because she is fed up with washing and embalming corpses.

(kořená jana, locker no. 26, natural death)
Maybe in my next to next life...
(recorded by nurse on duty katka, hospital coordinator nurse)
 ... she'll go having a beer with the other two
(...more and more...)
beautiful tall blonde ladies,
(...new suspected...)
for celebrating together
(...still spreading...)
another love story
(...a homeless, a wretch, some poet...)
and another professional achievement

(...natural death....)

(...natural death....)

(...natural death....)

Mircea Dan Duta. Prague, Czechia.

DAISY CHAIN

We met at the after-school book club,
two geeks in a pod.
When she spoke, I was rapt;
watching her talk with her hands,
gesturing enthusiasm for Mallory Towers;
seeing her talk with her eyes,
how they sparkled for Anastasia Krupnik.

Too young to understand
why I needed to be near her.
I wanted, so badly,
to invite her for tea,
share my toys,
show her the books I slept with -
my paper-scented teddy bears.

Primal instinct prodded me,
discouraged me, as though it knew
this wasn't normal.
A sandpit of confusion.

A tummy of worms and butterflies,
ladybirds and dragonflies.
My throat, a gobstopper lump

as we sit, at the back
of the school field,
shaded by evergreen pines,
the screeching of happy, football-playing
kids floating by on the wind.
She talked about why George
was better than Dick or Julian.

I plucked daises, and pierced holes
in their stems with nimble
8 year old fingers,
threaded daisy into daisy,
quietly wrapped the chain
around her wrist.
Ashley Edge, Stoke-on-Trent.
From their poetry collection "Those Days, These Days"

BEAULAH'S ADMONITION

(with gratitude to Carole King)

Be home when the street lights come on

it takes a long time

to dig a grave with a fork

there is no other way to remember

than putting names on a wall

be it the dark black one across the way

be it the chambers of your heart

be it scratchings in a cave

prepare for a lightning bolt

ride it til you feel

windswept
enthralled

between boulders
you might crash and burn
do not forget
that smoke rises
we are the hammer
the chisel
machete
and small knife

over yonder
your sweet tasting life
appears
beckons
flaps its wings dressed in fortune's clothing
makes the bed with linen sheets
hunkers down
leviathan roaming the wild

the web is woven by women
sisters will greet you when you arrive
be ready
be faithful
carry water

life will emerge
Sharon Elliott
Albuquerque, New Mexico USA

ORACLE

COME TALK…AND FAVOUR US…SO ABUNDANTLY

Sappho
fragment #27

as a sapling who's wood
is, yet, still green, I bend
freely to your will
unto your sacred temple
I dedicate my chanting
and through song confess
my longing for a fortune
yet untold
am I fated to take a lover
or, by misfortune, be betrayed?
robe me in your kindness
arouse in me your nightingale
that I might woo her to my bed
and pluck there the moon's
jealousy and ride my lover's
chariot to the golden shores
of dawn

Tim Evans. San Diego, Ca. USA.

DEAR FATHER TIME

even as a child you were a shitty dad
coming home late and smelling like blue cheese
with new life forms growing in your beard   mumbling
 what shall we do with the drunken sailor
 put him in the bed with the captain's daughter

i remember the role model you weren't
you never took me to the ballgame of saints
you never once rewarded me with a stop
freeze the world like a pause in a video
and let me walk around in your shoes

i didn't care   i was too busy becoming
ripe and sexual   taking my fair share in the marketplace
and you just   like   vanished for sixty years
did you take a shave   run off with some hotty nymph
abandon mother time who got too obese
and had to be carried around by four elements
earth water fire (and i forget the other)
before she collapsed drunk
with her face in a plate of spaghetti

and now you've come back
wanting to make amends
a decrepit man with arthritic wings
sitting next to me on the park bench
listening to serenades for strings
carrying an hour glass like a bongo drum

after you visited my biological mom and dad
and so many friends i loved

but still a father is a father
and even though you suck at it
i know you were watching every move i made
so proud of your cutie *zies-a-boy-a-lah*
pretending you don't exist

and i've been spending my inheritance
for more years than i can count
the heir apparent to the kingdom of time
at the roulette wheel of being in limbo
winning some and losing some
until all the money is gone
Mark Fishbein. Chicago,USA

ATOMIC WHIPLASH

You know how in cop shows,

when a house is booby trapped with explosives,

people get out just in time to not be blown up

but just in time to be thrown into the air from the front steps:

then, they always rise from the ground (usually) with minor injuries.

In real life, when someone get thrown by explosive force
they will likely need at least a neck brace for the whiplash.

When I met you, the second you walked away,
my body flew an unknown amount of miles.

You were an atomic bomb that blew up in my heart.

The emotional whiplash of the infatuation I suffered
slammed my heart against the walls of my psyche

as if you were a fishhook dipped in worm smoothie
and I was an unsuspecting catfish who recently
rose from the muck and mire of the riverbed.

You were my savior walking on water
making me jump in the air to greet you
till my gills needed resuscitation.

When you allowed me back in the water,
(unbeknownst to me) you had tuned water to wine,
leaving me in a drunken existence lest I try to breathe air
which is not advantageous to a catfish,

but at least,
if I ever eat an actual worm on an actual hook,
whoever grills me up
will have a catfish steak marinated in wine
with notes of infatuation and whiplash.

Generalissimo Bryan Franklin. Brunswick, Maine, USA

WHAT'S UP WITH THE GEESE IN DELAWARE?

When they're not "Up in the Air,"
they're on the ground, hundreds of them—
I've seen many a goose convention.

Hmmmm, geese must be very political folk,
or maybe they're exchanging Tupperware?

At any rate, they're traffic stoppers who waddle
across any highway, *single file*, slow as you like.

Don't geese fly south anymore? This winter
I watched from our Ogletown back deck

as hundreds of geese in wavering V-formations
flew north. . . I need to scour the news

—maybe a new casino has opened
on the Brandywine and the geese are flocking
to get to the card tables and roulette wheels.

Yes! I believe that must be it!
I hear their voices on the breeze
calling out, "*Gamble! Gamble! Gamble!*"
Christopher T. George. Newark, Delaware. USA

A HAME IS A HAME , IS IT NAE?

Efter Robert Seatter wae a nod tae Gertrude Stein for the title

Aa come fae Bothies and Strathspey, ma Grunny nicknamed Billy,

fa aa wish hid taught mi Gaelic as weel as Doric,

Aa come fae wirds, nae nummers,

fae "it's not fit, it's what" an

"pit on yer sheen an get doon tae at skweel, yer gan tae be late!"

Aa come fae three primaries and twa academies,

fae Mastrick backies an the braes o Hatton –

these placeys relate tae me bit they are nae ma hame.

Aa come fae Babysham an Blue Lagoons,

Advocaat an Lemonade lang afore the legal age,

fae different days – smokin in bairns faces,

hunners o tabbies in ashtrays thick as bricks,

enough tae burst yer skull crimson.

Aa come fae bleezin for a fortnecht

an the Dons European Cup Winners Cup song

weel efter midnecht, on repeat, for years.

Aa come fae kennin aa the wirds tae songs aa hate
an wid nivver choose tae listen tae.
Aa come fae Nerdsville, fae pages o sci-fi an fantasy buiks
orra wae bein used as escape pods,
gatewyes tae warlds aa sarely wished wis hame.

Aa come fae the 80s,
Neighbours, aabody loves gweed Neighbours,
fae Bros an Grolsch bottle tops on yer docs,
fae dyin aathin ye ain blaik an becomin a Goth.
Aa come fae the kaleidoscopic blur o the 90s,
fae raves, heidy wikkends, buggy flares,
hame-made tie-dye glow in the dark claes,
fae fitba taps an trackies, trekkin roon the city
hinkin ye couldnae be ony cooler
wae soonds blarin oot the ghettoblaster on yer shooder
an these attempts tae belang are part o fa aa am,
bit temporary phases dinnae signal hame.

Aa come fae graft and debt, swingin in atween extremes,
fae nae darin tae deek above the station
that's been hemmered intae yer heid
ats nae for you bairn, ats nae for me.

Aa come fae fit we're telt is hame,
aa lee we're selt fae fan we're wee –
hame exists in mortar an bricks,
flags an borders, Ikea furniture
flooery tablecloots laid oot aa bonnie
in yer fairmhoose style kitchen,

Mither makkin breid wearin a funcy apron,
at image is fiction, an illusion
for far too mony an we're led tae believe
if we've nae enough money tae get it
summin's wrang wae us if we dinnae hae it,
must nae be graftin hard enough, ay?
At is definitely nae hame.

Aa come fae dein a 180,
fae brakkin unwritten rules
an learnin tae trust yer ain journey.
Aa come fae livin in the moment
an slowin doon enough tae hear the unswers,
an they come, listen..
spaces that mak ye feel safe - hame
electric seconds afore the moshin stairts – hame
cooriein intae clean beddin – hame
ma nephew laughin an singin – hame
atein an bletherin wae ma freens – hame
the wye she felt in ma airms yon day - hame
watchin the lungs o the warld breathe in an oot in waves – hame
roamin aboot in the pishin rain – hame
readin yer ain scrievens on stage – hame
aa yon time lookin ootside, tae realise
it's here, yer hert's yer compass,
hame's a feelin, nae a hing
ye cairry it wae ye
farivver ye ging
Jo Gilbert. Aberdeen.Scotland.

AWFUL CONFUSION

She sits like my mum. Sat on a chair by a bed. She sits as though she was deep in thought, gently patting a crease on her neat check skirt. On her bedside cabinet, alongside untouched fruit and chocolate, from a dark wood frame bright young eyes laughing beam, in faded fifties sepia new lovers happy being.
And here, she sits alone, her life's love gone. One of few remaining of the bright young of that greatest of generations. Of those who saw the rise and fall and rise of tyrants. Watched Europe war then unite then divide. Felt the chill shiver of a cold world on the brink. And in a blink a life lived. And reward for those few left, to depart this earth to a lonely scared covid death.
And here, sat old in this cold ward, to heal, I pray. That same face that same smile. But from a sadness in her eyes, I saw she wanted hard to know me. And as we sat with our hands clasped tight. Face to face, son to mum, mum to son. From the depths of that once crystal mind, with a strength born of strength, in a voice as clear as a cold blue sky.
My gone dad's words uttered in my mum's sweet voice "I won't give up. We don't give up. I won't give up. We don't give up". A mantra for a life. That will to live born of love. Love given and received. Love that drags the soul from dark despair. And even in that awful confusion a love that never can be taken

Martin Goldie. Dunoon. Scotland.

1980 JUNETENTH UPRISING.

I'm walking down this hot street.

I'm holding a baby walking down this hot street.

I don't know why I'm doing this yet,

I'm thinking I'm just doing my job,

I'm a park leader, a skinny white girl,

on this second ever Juneteenth Parade in Austin, Texas,

celebrating the day the slaves heard they were free.

I mean I know why we're doing it—

I work at a park, two parks,

one all the kids are black,

one is mixed race.

But it hasn't really dawned that the heat of this march
is not just the sweat of my arms, the sweat of this child,
who is black,
not just our sweat sliding over each other,
intermingling and dropping, sizzling on the brutal street,
as the drums come solemn behind us.

It hasn't even dawned that the need of this child
is not just that this child's mother is at work,
not just that this child is a defenceless infant,
as the drums come solemn,
as the drums come solemn, come solemn.

We're marching down this hot street,
a gaggle of kids between three park leaders
all squinting into the sun,
almost nobody watching from the side-lines
'cause this ain't Congress Avenue.

This street is a backside to ugliness
between the Villa Capri Motel parking lot
and the Lyndon Baines Johnson Presidential Library parking lot.
A street radiating heat, cooking us like stew.
But we march on, this baby and I.

We made it, sister, and you never complained.
At nine months you knew,
it's taken me 59 years.

Today, I'm marching down this hot street,

I'm marching down this hot street with you.

Laura Grevel, Austria

Poem previously published on Poets Against Racism & Hate USA website, June 2023

COLLECTOR OF WORDS

I am a word collector, a collector of words,
from the ones most common, to others, quite absurd
I put them down on paper, and file,
And jots and notes, in lines
And in my thoughts
It's not a haiku, an epitaph or prose
it's my decision where each word goes.
Lyrical, sonnet, concrete or ekphrastic
verbally or aurally,
All of it fantastic
It's not a villanelle, tanku or rhyme
Just a collection of words,
Sometimes in order
And not in other times
Alliteration of literacy?
But that is my choice
A limerick?
Cinquain?
An ode?
Think I will pass,
It's not quite my voice.
Bordering close to the margin
The font doesn't matter

From the first to the last.
 Be it a ghazal, or an epic
One line or two
Epigram, acrostic,
Pen, black or blue
I'm collecting some words
How about you?
Sestina, verse, free or blank
I'm storing the words
In a secure word bank.
Pantoum, and others
Write it all down.
Save it.
Store it.
Never ignore it.
Big up to the long ones
Verbose or verboten
I'll not come up short
Some words long forgotten
Nouns, verbs, adverbs and more
Pronoun, prepositions, interjections
Huh.
Stop.
Now I'm just listing.
Yep.
That's for sure
Do I sense fensiveness?
Thanks for your support
I'll keep on collecting
I will not abort
I am a word collector
A collector of words.
Fin Hall New Pitsligo, Scotland

IMAGE OF DEATH

Bleary eyed I wake
At 3am
Nose running
Coughing
Covid
Feel sorry for myself
Put dressing gown on
Go downstairs make a drink
A hot beverage
To calm and comfort me
Feel very sorry for myself
Turn on BBC news
Film of burnt out car
See what looks like black log
By side of a burnt out car
It was a young man
Who had been trying to flee
His wedding ring showing
Against the black char of his hand
Flee with his family
Civilians
Who had screamed at Russian troops
Who they were
Not military
Just refugees
No longer feel sorry for myself

A droid had been filming
Their pleas were seen
The young wife is dead in the car
Also charred and burnt black
Head thrown back, mouth open
In a scream, like a scene from a horror film
Somehow their baby survived and was whisked away
Before the soldiers returned
And burnt the car and bodies
In attempt to disguise their crimes
Vile murder of the innocents
No lingering of pity for myself

Lots of evidence filmed

Of a Russian Army camp nearby
Loads of mess left as the Russians left
And the road littered with dead civilian corpses
All burnt this way

This is plain murder
This is war crime
This is vile
And I am lucky to go to bed
With Covid but no expectation of death
Richard Harries. Withersea England.

HIS WORK

a hand on a saw
one generation gone
a hand like mine
on wood
working the grain

this is work
time would have abandoned
long-fallen timber fallen twice
into disrepair
disregarded
failing
the hand stilled
and set aside

this is work
of more than an afternoon
the slow deciphering of invention
the self-sufficiency of war-years'
make-do and mend
its meticulous rebuilding
a door
a sneck
a copper strike-plate
a contrivance of blocks
closing the door
keeping it closed

this is work
late in the day wood-rot coming on
jambs like nine-pins stiffness seized
in the latch bolt click
step and tread weakened by an eternity
in the reckoning of an age of yesterdays
asking whose hand now will make
the old wood good and remember
the spirit of dead trees and wry design
whose hand to turn the same trick
winding function out of necessity
form out of fragments of a world
once broken

so I remade his door into tomorrow
fifty years and more after the first work
as if this tomorrow might yet be the better for it
I beat the copper plate and nailed the nails again
I shaped the wooden blocks
to click the lock
to snare the sneck
to hold the frame
where all of us go into rooms
as if going would be easy
as if closing a door would be easy
as easy as metal and wood
in an agile hand
making the world work as it needs to work
Brian Hill, Forres, UK

Previously published on my personal blog at
https://onepieceaweek.blogspot.com/2015/09/plane-of-memory.html

RED CLAY SLIP

As a slow horse drags you beyond
the periphery of my vision,
I panic at the vanishing of the sun
Some owl (Minerva?) calls into deepening dusk
as the rabble rises to imminent ruin.

Somehow, people think they can manage
the weight of a corpse in a large wooden box,
but they're banking on baked earth and still nerves,
not the red clay slip the rains brought today,
and not the enervation that comes with grief.

But the bodies always end up in the ground,
anyway, so what does it matter?
We look up, but no hope lives in the clouds.
But somehow, for some reason, these rough
beasts continue their shuffle to the East.

And the miracle of birth is just as shocking
as the diagnosis was, and we are trapped
in a samsara spiral as the dead retreat into
the earth and light annihilates peace,
until we find our nominal egress.

Randy Horton.New Mills, Derbyshire

TRUE LOVE

The heart has to shine, not hide.
When I breathe, tectonic plates shift
Deep inside.

Water wrinkles with light and wave forms.
Ocean and lake, silver rivers all
Lap the shore. New Zealand blues.
We are all home under the same sky, same Sun. Breathe in light and darkness. They
are equal.

Bumblebees are sleeping still, as true Spring has not arrived. On midsummer
mornings, I found them sleeping in the flowers.

The universe is a system of systems, language of languages. Every atom, every
molecule sings its song. We only have to listen deeply to translate a new ancient
rhythm. Liquorice midnight sky abounds with infinite stars.

Spirits of bumblebees visit us. Remind us. Respect instead of poison. Crickets out of synch would never happen. They sing the bright world all night.

Nature of freedom. Freedom of Nature.
Music of the Spheres is true reality.
Industrial magnates long forgotten
Moral centers. Pull out from the planet what profits them. No respect. No respect!
Austerity for most while some get rich. It's gotta flip.

Heart song. Love songs that are true.
Frogs orbit the Moon when they dream, in and out of water and science. Water sustains us. We are made of it.

We poison our love, our water, only to hurt ourselves. Consuming the Earth.
Nurturing the Earth as good stewards instead. Sweet animals we eat instead of revere.
How do we speak this world into a better existence? What is the spell that stops brainwashing the status quo?
She is equine. She leads us. It should be women and children leading us to
True love, after all…
Amy Hoskins. Nashville. USA

WHERE HAVE ALL THE FLOWERS GONE?

Once the gift of flowers grew wild and free,
Giving unconditional love to you and thee
Marinating all the senses, to smell, to heal and hear,
To illuminate and see, to forgive the heart and to treasure the bee
Where have all the flowers gone

Trampled from blossoming,
Buttercups are closing
Poppies are not remembering
No seeds are sowing
Where have all the flowers gone
We are now our own crop circles,
Round and round with nowhere to go
No burning candles to blow,
Where have all the flowers gone,

Do they lay by the fallen?
Do they say I love you?

Do they speak in silence?
Who knows?
Where have all the flowers gone
In the land of fruit and honey
Where have Martin, Nelson, and Harriet gone
I still smell their enticing aroma, but why can't hear their flowers sing
As the cycle of life turns, crowns of thorns come and go,
The blossoms of life stay eternal,
Though it is planted in stone
Our seed must grow

Let us be the light
Together with flowing water
Our seed will blossom and grow

  Let us be the light
  By saying no to injustice
  And yes to fair play
  Be a caregiver not a troublemaker
  be a torch bearer

Let us be the light
Pour premium H20 out of our golden pales
cleansed of pain
Where there was peace and tranquility,
Where no one hold their heads in shame
Where the flowers blossom inside you and me
Woven into life' tapestry

With a proud, glorious ancestry
It is time to set our children free
Let them play in a brave new garden
The dream continues, not just Martins emancipation
It is all our proclamation
Gary Huskisson. Peterborough. England.

POETS' WORLD

This is the story of the master year

This is the story of love
This is the story of wisdom
This is the story of the price above
The story of rottenness in bone
I live in the world of the poets
Where the story of the world is the story of more
The story of abundance
Running rivers reckless remorse
As the poets live and will tell it
Better grander sweeter softer
Ending tragic in broken black and darkness darkest
Opening and turning towards is what the poetry is for
Opening and turning towards is what the living life is for
This where I am
where I prefer to stay
here rubies here gold
blossom for asking
These words told treasures in the hearts and souls
The world of the poets accepting all that comes with
The price above
Whispers on lips
A rainbow of rubies. The multitude
The ocean
The forest
The mountain
The earth
The stars
The galaxies
The nebula
Cannot obscure

The pucker

The nectar of love's goodnight kiss

The sorrow that grips

The dark light we cannot we cannot cannot see

The shading

the nuance black white and gray

The spectrum of rainbow unseen

Where scientist play with gear and gizmos

Who is the wiser in the world of the poets

The inventors of words not yet known

The words in numbers so large

It takes days and days

Of tracing the zeros on the infinite torus

To come even close to counting them all

I will trade a day in the world of poets

For years in Valhalla or heaven or

Towns of fluffy clouds

Or in circus tents with cotton candy candy clowns

I found in the world of poets my soul

My heart my love

Love in every sense of the word

From babies on breasts

To wild animal growls

The world of poets is my home

Better than rubies and all things desired

From the knowledge of lips the knowledge

Of the meaning of a virtuous woman who is in the world of the poets a poet

Worth more than and far above the price of rubies

Dane Ince. San Francisco, California, USA

UNTITLED

You have moved me with your moves.

Let me walk in your shoes. At least in your thoughts.

Let me stumble, and stumble back to you,

and to your thoughts.

Will you catch me, when I fall

like big snowflakes at noon

into your sky-grey eyes in the dimmed bedside light

sharing stories without saying a single word?

Hold me
like you hold your thoughts.
Let me be closer to wherever you keep them.
Let me leave, and leave that meaningful pause,
filled with your thoughts.
Will you shine the light in the dark -
with your beacon-bright smile
like a rising full moon, painting its silvers to the sea
silently singing on the sandy shores beneath us?

Birgit Itse, Aberdeen via Estonia

JOURNEY OF INSCAPES

A door to the past opens
a dream wrapped in wings
in the scattershot light of dawn
beyond the far side of the stars

A journey of inscapes begins
a summation of past present and future
amid memories never made
and shifting shapes of shadows

Shadows of time and place
reflecting refracting into infinity
an infinity of rememory

and a longing for what never was

Songs of saudade and hiraeth
echo among stars and galaxies
resound through the Multiverse
ancient ariose cantos of loss and longing

Life and existence are
everywhere and everywhen is
as shores of being are stravaged
and I Am
Doc Janning. South Euclid, Ohio,USA

PEAKS

When you need a place of solace
you can find me without a map

I rise above the horizon
my virtues are visible from a distance

and through the mists they shine
you can tread the mossy soft path
of least resistance into my domain

I have many names, my wisdom
as layered and steadfast as the time
that weathered my rocky outcrops raw

my pain is dissipated through my many
seeping channels and my wounds are always open

my leaking hurt is not harmful but healing
because the feeling reforms as dew
every morning dawning realisations anew

this is the mountain of
everlasting unconditional love
for everything about you
Kate Jenkinson. Doncaster, England

EPIGRAPH #1: "Who knew hindsight could really be blind" - AJ Houston

In response to one of the many things that are labeled blind, colorblindness used to be where everything was looked at as grey monotone. Certain colors were indistinguishable from others. When referring to people, it has a different connotation. Colorblind can refer to a person who is not aware of cultural disparities and turns a blind eye to this by refusing to acknowledge the fact that it exists. Two weeks ago the house next door to me caught on fire. The families got out OK but everything in the house was destroyed by smoke. The families stood out in the street all day waiting for the fire to be put out and for the Red Cross to come and take them to a hotel. Last night I heard gunshots. Today I heard screaming. A man is still screaming outside right now.

Terri Rose Jertson.Wanaque, New Jersey. USA

A OFF-THE-BEATEN-PATH TOUR OF CENTRAL PARK

"Thank you, everyone, for coming on our tour of Central Park. I'm your tour guide Dudley Do- What? and I'll be assisted by Scout. He's wearing an Eagle Scout uniform plastered with every badge in the book. Good job, Scout.

"As you know, we're going to explore things most tour guides overlook. Yes, folks, these won't make it into Frommer's!

"We'll enter the park here ... and on our left is our first tour stop. If you look closely under this bush---I don't know what kind it is! Not important!---you'll see a collection of excrement. The local lingo would be 'shit.' I don't know what kind of animals made this! It's a curiosity find!!

[Dismayed] "I see a couple of people are peeling off from the tour already, but don't let that discourage you. [Saying it to himself, hands to head.] The rest of us will forge ahead. Go on.

[Tour guide to Scout, sotto voce]: "Scout, did you put the bird in place? ... [apoplectic] You got a rubber chicken?! It was supposed to be road kill! ... Well, all right, put it in place, and hurry.

[Tour guide aloud to tour]: "Ok, people, look over here to the right! It's a ... a two-winged butterfly! No, I don't know what kind! What's important is it's two-winged! Jot it down!

"Now, up here on the left---ah, Scout, there you are--- People, if you could squat to get under these branches... Whoops, that branch just slapped you right in the face! Don't worry; Scout has Flintstone bandages; people often get injured on our tours.

"So under these branches we often find---yes, there's one now---a flattened, well, that is, a bird carcass. No, don't touch! Yes, they often have that sickly yellow shade right after the death pallor kicks in. I don't know how this bird met its demise!---[snarky] a one-hundred-ton gorilla?---but it can't have been pleasant. Oh... I see a couple of [snarky] 'birdwatchers' have left our group. But the rest of us will continue on! [Angrily, sputtering, fists clenched.] Mmm!! [Then deep breath to try to calm down.] "On your right is the Delacorte Theatre, where 'Shakespeare in the Park' is staged. My God. Must be a mistake in our itinerary. [Angrily.] It's like a regular tour stop!! [Snappish] Well, sure, go ahead and take a photo, but then we must be off to our next planned tour stop!!

"Ahead is a spot where, historically, many people have crossed the road. I don't know how many or whether any chickens were among them! But for many years, people were crossing over this piece of land.

[deep breath] "I see we've lost a few more people, back at the [snarky] 'Delacorte,' still taking pictures---including Scout!! Well, no one else get injured, ha ha! Yes, the three of us will carry on.

"The [snarky] 'Delacorte Dilettanti' will miss the highlight of the tour! Let's see, is this the right tree? [Taps on it.] Yes. If you stand under this particular evergreen and look up really high, tilt your head, shade your eyes, yes, you can see it now. It's not always visible, but when the light hits in a certain way (nice when it happens during

Tour Time), you can see the sunrays splaying through the branches. Now's the time to take pictures! Ah, you just can't put a price on nature, eh?

"But you can put a price on this tour. [Takes off hat, holds upside down, extends it and moves it in half-circle and back.] Thank you for your prepayment, but any tips you'd like to make now would be especially welcome. Our expert guidance comes at a cost to stay abreast of the latest unique happenings in the park, and we always strive to provide a tour unlike any other. Oh, thanks. [Sarcastically] I needed more quarters for laundry. Thank you. And thanks, a greenback! [Grabs a $1 bill out of hat, holds it up to the light to check that it's good, then stuffs it into pocket.]

"Don't forget the names Dudley Do-What? and Scout, for the best in Off-the-Beaten-Path tours of Central Park.

[Sweeps hat in a bow.] "Good day." [Puts hat back on and walks away, muttering "Don't let the tree hit you in the ass on the way out".]

Merilee Johnson,New York

THE JUSTICE OF BULLETS FOR CROWD CONTROL

I AM DEAD
Words thrown at your face
bullets shot into my head
attack dogs keep me in place
it's okay if I end up dead

EVIDENCE IS DEAD
mourn me virtual distant eyes
see the red holes in my chest
lips spit out their old dusty lies
show the body-cam on the vest

MY CHILD IS DEAD
a grieving mother's tears rain down
father's hands try to lift his child still
as blood fills the cracks in the ground
outlined chalk lines drawn to reveal

THEIR EYES ARE DEAD
we're looking for another way
find new paths of Freedom's dream
outpouring loud words we say
WE'RE HUMAN! Hear our scream.
Henry L. Jones. Hendersonville, TN

PEACETIME

When I was born children were being flayed in Nam,
Then it was Cambodia, Somalia, Sudan,
And all that time Israelis were killing Arabs in spades,
Little wars in the tropics, forays and raids.

I grew up with war on the news every day,
And yet this was peacetime, or that's what they say.

Then liberation from tyranny were the words of the season,
Still innocents suffered in Bosnia against reason,
It was the end of history declared Fukuyama,
An end to battle, to strife and all of that drama.

And the war was still on the news every day,
And yet this was peacetime, or that's what they say.

Then it was war against drugs, and war against terror,
Fighting nouns and chemicals could be said to be error,
And back to real war against Saddam Hussein,
They enjoyed it so much, they fought him again.

And the war on the news showed hundreds of dead,
And yet this was peacetime, or that's what they said.

Vicious conflict in Syria with so many bad actors,
Assad, Isis, Russia, CIA – all were factors,
Then Yemen exploded with Saudi bought bombs,
If you thought that was enough, I'm afraid you were wrong.

The war on the news did not go away,
And yet this was peacetime, or that's what they say.

And the war in Ukraine brings us bang up to date,
A real war in Europe, state against state,
It appears to be something that boys like to achieve,
To fight for their countries, or for what they believe.

And so there is war on the news every day,
And yet this is peacetime, or that's what they say.

They're fighting for democracy, fighting for truth,
Fighting for god, and they're fighting for youth

And they'll fight and they'll fight until everyone's dead.

And yet it was peacetime, or that's what they said

Gareth Joseph. Cardiff, Wales

SHADOWS OF INJUSTICE

In a world where darkness looms with might
Where hearts are weary and souls take flight
There lies a plea, a passionate cry
To cease the pain, to let love defy

Stop the violence that tears us apart
Let compassion ignite a flame in every heart
For in this world, we're all connected
By the same thread of life, we're protected

In the shadows, the innocent weep
Their tears, a river, so vast and deep
Hear their plea, their silent screams
Resounding through the void, shattered dreams

In Nottingham, where stories unfold
A chilling tale waiting to be told
Of people lost in shadows deep
Their spirits wandering, unable to sleep

Once, vibrant lives filled this ancient town
Now mere whispers, their voices drowned
Gone are the laughter and the song
Replaced by sorrow, a haunting throng

Oh politicians, with honeyed words that drip from your tongues
Promising change, but delivering only crumbs
You dance with corruption, in a twisted romance
Leaving the people disillusioned, without a chance

In the corridors of power, where secrets lie

You make deals behind closed doors, with a sly and cunning eye
Laws are mere playthings, to be bent and twisted
While the voices of the people are ruthlessly resisted

In the shadows where darkness resides
A tale of corruption, where truth hides
A dance with power, a game of disguise
Where the righteous yearn for justice to rise

Once noble guardians, symbols of law
The police, they stood tall with valour and awe
But as the shadows grew longer each day
They found themselves lured astray

In lands afar, where shadows dance
A tale unfolds, a war's advance
Where eagles soar, in skies so vast
A storm brews, the die is cast

Ukraine's heart, a nation proud and strong
Their spirit unyielding, their will, resolute for long
But Russia, a mighty force, with power untamed
Seeks to conquer, to dominate, to leave Ukraine maimed

Racism, a beast that gnaws at our souls
Feeding hatred into the mouths of trolls
Dividing us based on the colour of our skin
Ignoring the beauty that lies within

Sexism, a poison that infects our minds
Limiting opportunities, leaving dreams behind
Judging abilities based on gender
Ignoring talent and potential, causing surrender

Disability discrimination, a heartless injustice
Denying equal rights, leaving scars that persist
Judging based on what one cannot control
Depriving them of dignity, taking a toll

But in the face of adversity, we stand tall
Unyielding, united, breaking down the walls
For we are warriors, resilient and strong
Fighting against prejudice, righting the wrong

D K. Atherstone, England

YES GIRL

 I am not a "yes" person.

I don't and won't tell you what I think you want to hear…
and getting to that point was a JOURNEY.

Because I didn't used to value me.
Because I used to think the only way people would like or accept me

was if I agreed with everything they said,
if I didn't have my own opinions
or make waves with my questions…
I guess you could say, I've been liberated.

Set free-

though there was no great time marking moment for me to say-
this is my Independence Day…

With freedom and friendship comes great responsibility.
To which I accept the challenge
And daily rise to it.
I am not a yes kind of girl…

And in constantly seeking to achieve my greatest destiny,

I realize I'm exactly right for this world.
I am ally and I am friend.
I am support system- you can talk it out with me.

But I am not a yes girl

So do not set your expectations for me to be exactly what you want to hear…

Because I am not a yes girl.

But isn't that exactly what is needed

In order for actual conversation, understanding and growth to happen;
So that biases built like giant walls designed to keep everything looking exactly the same

Can be torn down? Weeded out?
I am the revolution.
I am yassss Queen!

I am smiles and laughter.
I am if we build it they will come.
I am light from the sun-

It's energy radiates through me, exploding upon anyone within my aura.

But.
Be ye forever warned-
I am not a yes kind of person.
Special K. Richmond Virginia, USA.

CALIFORNIA

in California they'll be planting oranges,

it's something to think about on a wet Sunday afternoon -

if the weather clears we can walk down to the broken pier

and watch the seagulls land beyond the keep-out sign -

it makes you think why all those dustbowl folks

traipsed out of deserts towards the sun,

makes all the newscast-reels and Guthrie songs

that whistle out of cinemas and crackly speakers

sound obvious – now, when I see a muddy shore

and questing sky beyond some one-arm bandit store,

I invent, if I'm honest under my plastic cape and cap,

that thing for which America's become a proxy:

a Californian vista in which oranges grow effortlessly,

where John Wayne leans on his saddle hard,

encompassing humanity, bright and true,

the freedom-lie that all believers stumble to.

Gerald Kells, Walsall, England

Published by Lulu in '51 Poems'

THE CLIP

 The telephone exchange in Kenny MacKinnon's house,

with its churn of gossip, was our first barber's shop.

We'd not go for a haircut but a clip;

and that clip depended on your mother's instructions.

A bowl-shaped tidy-up,

or Kenny's preferred option, which eliminated mistakes,

a skull-scraping crew cut.

He got to work with the buzz of the razor,

like a jar of wasps, that you hoped didn't nick your ear,

listening for the snick, snick, snick of scissors,

as another chunk of hair slithered onto

the black cape that prevented your arms from

reaching up to scratch your nose,

the snick, snick, snick, of scissors were

interrupted only by Kenny's work at the switchboard.

Putting you through to Harris 2319,

and how's the weather in Kyle today,

Ciamar a tha thu?

Yes, we'll be shearing sheep here tomorrow.

Deisal 's deonach
We were never offered our option for the clip:
Just the slightest trim Kenny, we begged,
as we tried to cultivate shoulder-sweeping locks,
and the coolness of Beatlemania.
Buzz,buzz, snip, snip, snip.
Yes, another crew-cut,
Cool, but not in the way we wanted .
Bob Kenyon, Aberdeen Scotland.

COLOR

Drawing picture of what it looks like bigger.
Picture This
As you close your eyes imagine the beautiful plan God created
Picture This
The nice people gentle matters
Picture This
The twist, the turn and pull of getting together what seems different.
Picture This
The hiding, seeking, and funding is bringing remembrance to what people believe.
Picture This
As the handwriting is on the wall justice bring to stop
Picture This
As one season close, to another one adventure, to level speed and moving forward.
Picture This
Tap the water, to the trees and bridges high level.
Picture This
The picture as a bigger play
Picture This

Keyana The Artist . Atlanta.Georgia, USA

ENVIRONMENTAL OVERLOAD

This is a serious message to our human race.
We are losing ground literally and even air.
Warning: Environmental Overload.
We humans are killing our environment.
Environmental protection clubs are everywhere but
We still have pollution and global warming at an alarming rate.
Taking time to care for our bodies also means
We must care for the environment.
Take a glass of water from the tap and test it.
What do you see as a result?
Can you tell it tastes different than when you were
A child drinking from a fountain?
The city air has a smell and makes asthma worse.
The temperature is changing all over the globe.
We see landscapes changing, too many buildings, hazy skies.
Can we take a moment environmentally
To make a change in the way we live?
Can we find it in our hearts and minds to think of
How are we leaving Earth for our future children?
We must do something every day to fight back.
Implementing rules are tough and
Most of the population disregards rules.
We must learn to recycle and reuse the things we put in landfills.
There are places in the world
Where communities have been taught how to deal with trash.
Many of us have recycle bins in our neighborhoods
Yet we forget how to use them properly.
Next time you buy something, think about where it will end up.
This is a new kind of thinking that will heal our planet and
Stop our environmental overload.
Franchesa Kirkpatrick. Nashville. USA

LIGHT SWITCH

On…
I wake up to a gloomy day, every now and then
to see a flicker of light peeking through the curtain gap,
like the light is playing hide and seek.

Off…
I dream about waffles the next morning,
the smell creeping up my nose.
I won't even bother to turn the light switch on,
and before I know it, I'm back up in the pitch black of my
universal dream, flicking the light switch on again.

On…
I wake up to the bright screen of my phone
as the annoying alarm goes off.
It's still dark outside so I go to turn my light on,
but nothing happens.

Off…
The light won't work because there's a power outage.
I check my watch to see what time it is but it is flat. Urgh!
(A) - the light won't work, (B) - I have no idea what time it is,
and now I tripped over the shoes I left out.
I pick up my phone and see a message saying,
"Warning - battery is low." My phone then shuts down.
I get up forgetting I moved into a new house and walk blindly into a wall.
I made a dent. Two actually. One on my head and the other in the wall.
I can see it now because the light Is playing hide and seek again,
this time for a while.

On…
Finally, I can see again, and I won hide and seek
because the light was behind the curtains I opened earlier.

Off…
I fall to sleep dreaming about some weird incinerator thing
that I'm climbing into for some reason… It's Hot!

On…
I wake to the smell of waffles and chocolate ice cream.
Well, I can't smell the ice cream, but I know it's there.

I float to the kitchen knowing which is biggest and choose it.
Waffles, my dream.

Off…
My dreams like the universe come alive
as I think about the past, wonder about the present,
and imagine the future.
Elijah Khon. Adelaide. Australia

EXCURSION EXTINCTION

I got lost on a school excursion at the national park.
Fear comes over me, I need to find my class before day turns to dark.
Carefully stepping, carefully listening for any sound they make.
Looking for my class between the trees so I can again be safe.

I hear a loud thump, thump, thump coming from behind me.
I turn, crouch, squint my eyes to see what I can see.
I slowly move toward the thump, stumble over and hurt my knee.
The biggest, strangest beast I've seen is staring back through the trees.

Feet like a lion, full of claws.
Legs like a leopard, fast and pouncey.
Arms like an octopus, grippy and wavey.
Body like a bear, broad and strong.
Teeth like a tiger, sharp and long.
Eyes like a wolf, piercing and wide.
Horn like a rhino, protecting its head.
Ears like a rabbit, pointy and tall.
Fur like a Husky, keeping it warm.
Colour of a bat, black as the night.
Tall as a giraffe, filling me with fright.

I go to get up and yell in pain, scream in fear.
The beast has seen me, and in two steps, it is so near.
Its octopus arms pick me up and fling me into the air.
Its tiger teeth catch me, I feel a chomp, land here, land there.

I'm lying here in blood...
Not quite dead yet but just
about dead. Yeah… Dead
Jadon Khon. Adelaide, Australia

VENI, VIDI, VULNERABILI

Vigilant… After what happened,
I never leave a drink alone,
never fully pack a bag,
always watch my back…

Visualise… Even in the negative,
I seek to see the positive.
In the missing of ones loved,
envision oneness…

Vocalise… I share my words
on the page and on the stage
to help others feel seen, heard,
understood, supported…

Void… There is a hole in my heart,
my soul, where people that mattered,
people that still matter, fit;
where only they fit…

Voyage… Life is a journey,
countless departures, countless destinations,
some calming, others numbing,
all important to my becoming…

Vulnerable… Important to me,
to others, risking it all as I live
in gratitude, in grace,
sharing the story I own…

Because no matter how hard some might try to steal my pen,
It's my story, and I am the only one who can write the ending
Paul Khon. Adelaide, Australia

A BLOT FROM THE BLUE 1 MIN 25 SECS

I was never good at painting, and would send
Splashes everywhere! My clothes were so full of
Stains, that my washing machine screamed from the
Quantity of stain-removers, that I used to wash my clothes.

Now I blot from the blue --tiny specks of ink-splattered
Words, scattered all over the robes, sanctum and mansions
Of the soul, calligraphing, with my pen or keyboard, the
Lapis-lazuli of the perennial heavens, in indigo-blue ink.

Yes, I splodge my imperfections, blemishes, and struggles, my
Joys and sorrows, on the Citadel of each Heart through poetry,
Using the gift of eloquence, to show that there is light in adversity…
That a blotter's speck-filled canvas, can also be a tapestry of Love.

I paint stains of beauty on the Heart, blots like a blue moon,
Not the ones that crowd my attire with blotches, but gives
A dazzling smile and a ray of sunshine to souls, longing for the
Light of a luminous dawn, and the lustrous splendour of sunrise.

Yes, I was never going to be a child prodigy at blotting, but Grace
Gave me, instead, the sweet bars of the poetic artist, not to create
A jig-saw puzzle of confusion, but a kaleidoscope of magnificence,
Rainbows of the Spirit, so enchanting, as to enthral the wonders of the soul.
Manatita, The Lantern Carrier. London, England

BURIAL IN SOIL. *3*

What is soil except

a community

that accepts what I

need help to bury?

Within soil, burrows

cocoon my sorrows.

Here all things spoken

sotto voce count.

Here the White Rabbit's
watch dictates the time,
says it's always right,
lots left, at the side.

I inhale deeply.
Unmistakable
soil scent, so earthy
with layered accents.

The underground gives
a diff'rent comfort
that's not what is found
in the aboveground.

My non-bionic
ears cannot fathom
the hertz (hurts) of other
frequency systems.

There is a darkness
that is teeming here.
Much is going on.
Perhaps I am wrong.

Have I been missing,
misinterpreting,
squinting right through these
maladjusted eyes?

The intangible
seems quite within reach.

Brand new discov'ry.

Still feels whimsical.

My hand reaches out,

tightly grasps the soil.

I feel a dampness

and shards of sharpness.

I let out a cry.

We both say goodbye.

Sotto voce. With:

"你走你的阳关道，我过我的独木桥"

(nǐ zǒu nǐ de yáng guān dào wǒ guò wǒ de wǒ de dúmù qiáo)[1].

I bury my head

in mee siam[2], mee pok[3],

fried rice, mee soto[4]

sans my hurts, solo.

Hurts buried in soil,

I go aboveground,

listen to the sounds.

The still shared sky smiles.

Jennifer Leong (Soy Avocado). Singapore

Digital Pulse

Security camera

stares and 50,000

eyes can see. Walk

down the road

and be an
instantaneous
anonymous celebrity.
Eyes crank
to see through
algorithmic hum.

What are you doing,
how are you today?

Catalog my interests
and be wary
of my thought
process. Assign a
code, flag a thought.
Freedom is
nobody's when
security blanket is
drawn to the bosom
and fear
mongers sell their
wares.

My 15 minutes of fame
are infinite!
~webcasts, podcasts,
social posts,
credit card transactions,
selfie picks~

Don't you want to
look at me?

Cherry pick my
thoughts. Here's
what I want you to
know about
me. Superhuman
today from
down in the gutter.
Click "like"
for instantaneous
gratification pat
on the back.

And everyone
watches on.
Drain my life down
circuitry
hidden behind the
walls.
Everything I want:
Sell me an ad.
Spy on my life.

I'm a limited edition
collectors
item for the highest
bidder, a

unique 100%
guaranteed human
individual in a pool
of millions.
And now I can buy
that shit that I
want and you can bag
and tag my
very thoughts.

I'll post about it
tomorrow.

**Noah Levin. New
York**.

tWHYLIGHT

i'm always a grandmother's boy
and you're ever a grandson's lady
but forever surprised us both
when i called your name

and silence was all you can give me
as sunlight became mute
under your complexion
every inch of skin, undisturbed

not a single bone, moved
my entire life, paused
from the screams my heart strung for
you, lay there like an unending second

that counted the gods i could deny
so no one could take the smiles
you only reserved for me
even for a while longer

we did say our goodbyes
between your coughs, and
my hand under your palm at 4am
i did release you, by holding on

but your exit didn't tell me—how
your how—came for me after breakfast
you always loved preparing that for me
but i will never enjoy may 28, 2008's

i've been hungry since that day
you left your breath with the night
and grief is the only one rising
whenever memories collect me

like how the white linen took you
and shapeless regret was born
of not saying i love you enough
today, exactly 15 years had passed

and all i can still say is... i love you
LKN. Philippines

OVERTHINKING

Overthinking once more and inside my head things are out of control

Thoughts are racing around and I cannot turn them off
Lying in bed it's 4.20am and sleep evades me again
I wish I could relax and stop thinking so much

Covid, Christmas, family, money, everyone's health, the weather ....
If I didn't have anything to worry about I'd fret
I guess it's just part of the job
Of mother, wife, sister, daughter, friend and confidante.

I'd hoped in middle age I could relax and put up my feet
But as the wrinkles get more plentiful and the hair so grey
I'll go with the hand I've been dealt and just accept
There's worse ways to live than being needed and required.
Caroline Low, Glenrothes, Fife, Scotland   Previously published. 14 July 2021 in
"Joined Up Writing; The Second Instalment:

THE WELL

As a child, I was afraid to go near,

It sang with a 'come hither' dark magic,

I could peer into its fathomless depths

And imagine myself trapped

Forever in some nether world,

A place of green, reflected sunshine,

The place from which

all primal things spring.

My father nailed iron

over the top, to keep

the bad things out,

But still, some nights,

I'd imagine them trailing

translucent tendril limbs

from the temptress water,

Where a thousand unblinking

reptilian eyes waited, in the dark,

To claim me as theirs.

I'd twist in my sheets,

Hearing the rumble

of underground voices,

Rattle of stone against stone,

Trailing wet footmarks

on the step.

Think of that cold, dark

magic pulling me in,

The irresistible tug of it,

The secret thrill of disobeying –

of even thinking it –

The cold, dark Nothing

That awaited me underground,

That called to me

That called to me,

Even though

I feared it.

Becky Lowe. Swansea.Wales

OLD WOMAN WITH A PHOTOGRAPH

My husband was fighting in Italy.
I have a photograph, him marching,
taken on the road from the beach.
I hadn't seen him for six months,
and didn't see him for another seven.

You were in London on a weekend pass.
I have a photograph, us dancing,
taken when my friends and I stepped out.
I'd never seen you before that evening,
and I never saw you after that.

I know the rest of my husband's story.
I have boxes of photographs, us laughing,
holidays with the children, their weddings.
He passed a week before turning eighty,
and my love for him is still as strong.

But of you, my handsome young Yank pilot,
I only have that photograph, us laughing.
A corner of my faithful heart is still yours,
no danger to my husband or our children,
and I think I'd rather that were all I know.
 Lennart Lundh. Chicago Illinois. USA
first published in *Write Like You're Alive* (Zoetic Press, 2016)

UNCONTACTED

a people at least
thirty thousand years old
living on what their island provides
naked, handsome, happy
(we imagine)
'uncontacted' – no,
uncontactable
by their own wish
which they enforce by attacking
anyone who tries to land

but we want to know about them
how they live, how they have survived
on an island of twenty-three square miles
for so many millennia:
can their needs be so modest?
have they solved the problem of overpopulation
in some way we might disapprove of?
has nature herself set limits
on their fecundity?

from time to time
we send emissaries, confident
we can help
we know what they want

they want Jesus
they want money
they want booze
they want pop music
they want the internet
but most of all, they want

cars
and Coke

some of our gifts
they use –
metal salvaged from broken ships
for arrowheads
bits of the brittle plastic tide we send
to slosh against their shores

just once
a boatload of coconuts
brought them down to their beach
in friendship, or truce
they like coconuts
but coconuts don't grow
on their island

everyone else
they drive off with yells
in their language that no-one else understands
and arrows
Mandy MacDonald. Aberdeen Scotland.
Previously published.

HOW NOW?

The distinct colours of sound
tumble in a rainbow through her mind
as she stumbles through life, forever forgetting
that each and every iota of fabric
covering her very limbs, is made of
the same atoms she herself is made of.

The reminders come, at the speed of light
to bombard her eyeballs and assault
the lining of her nostrils while she runs,
aware of how her skin is dying more every day.
The light fades as she nears the end
of the journey she undertook so many years ago.

The books, piled high, fight with the other

detritus of her familiar surroundings
only to confuse themselves with real people
she has known before.
The flash of lightening only serves to
Illuminate the facts strewn before her now.
Not all is as it seems, not all was as it looked before.

Her head swims with questions being
fired off at odd angles within her brain.
The smell of   something… burnt beyond recognition
sparks memories, despite being indecipherable, unrecognisable.
Faces and names, long lost to her
return in momentary flashes to entice her further.
Where to, and why? she wonders. How now?
Caroline Mackie, 28th March 2023 Edinburgh, Scotland (residing Almere,
Netherlands)
Previously 'published' on my own Facebook page 'Rantin Roarins'

LESS THAN

If I shower now -

will wash away all trace of you

If I shower now -

will remove your touch

Brushing teeth

will disappear the taste of you

Cleansing process

would be too much

Close my eyes -

I'd lose sight of your face

Open them -
you'd vanish without trace

Block my ears -
I would lose the choice

of listening for -
your voice

Once showering -
was all done

I would feel less -
than human

You make me -
so alive

without this -
can't survive

I would become -
Zombie-fied

As if my soul -
had died

Des Mannay, Newport, Gwent, Wales

WHAT REMAINS

black moon against a scarlet sky: on a desert
street, I am parched / my skin's
refrigerated—

shivering through siroccos of sand-filled
air, I crawl in place—an alternative
to migration: you appear—

we sit in the street and eat
desiccated figs: we drink
ice-water: salt crusts our lips—

what remains between us?

unless we can describe our remains, or
bury them, you / I / we
can never leave—

nakedness has not prepared me
to be silent—

un-homed: beyond our pale
imagining—what
remains but tenderness?

Jude Marr, Leominster, England. Originally published in *Oxidant Engi*

AMOR FATI
for my son Gabriel

Revolving in a twist of speeding time,
I ponder metaphysics obliquely.
In youth the only cause to make me rhyme
Was loving irresponsibility.
In age I wind the clock; the hours chime,
And travel back is easy. Travel forth?
A body buried deep in wormy slime,
Or spirit sailing on to its true north?

Resolving riddles seems impossible.
Existence is a book and, when it ends,
Perhaps the mystery seemed solvable
But then the book is shut. What this portends
Is chapter after chapter one must try
To savour deviance in narrative,
The twist of dialogue and wit and lie,
The pace, the plot and its imperative.

Perhaps description is the surest route
To transcendental apprehension's peace.
Adopt a passive mode and pause and, mute,
Attend to sounds strange outer worlds release.
Slight echoes through the scene as twilight dims,
Faint intimations hidden in a text,
Wild wonders agitated by weird whims,
Night flights aborted, prior and the next...

Or throw away the book and simply sit
And conjure up enchantments from the past
And find in them a patterning to fit
Fond early joys with what may be the last.
Discern that figure; take from it this faith:
A destiny is set; you can't do more
Than welcome certain future as a wraith.
Wise men can't know what else may be in store.

*

Imagine you could once get out of life
And, gazing back, begin to comprehend

The whole of then and now - the questions rife
From setting out in passion 'til the end.
Could you gain cosmic height, pure point of view,
The eagle's sight and cool, his inspection
Of everything below that scurries through,
Defying danger, blind to detection?

In nocturne flight, swoop down and upward wing
To soar on high, Elysium to skry,
And pass beyond, eternity to ring,
Existence in continuums of sky,
And time unbound by space, this age, this hour,
This little life, this hounded mortal phase
Of pain, anxiety and loss of power,
This failure of the word, that dying phrase?
Embarrassment. Regain empyrean!
The poet's bliss, a moment, youth's fresh face -
Oh god! one vision safe - oblivion
And ecstasy, to surge, to shriek, to chase.

*

Do eagles really care if they are seen?
Perhaps they welcome it. God's vanity
Is obscure to the human. What has been
Becomes at long last myth, old history.
In dreams we swoon, without an answer, dim
To intimations, ancient faiths unknown;
Quotidiana dense in which we swim
Occludes perception of the final home.

The eagle hardly cares, it would appear.
He has an eye of god, so fine aloft.
It's only close to earth that he must fear
Dark predators like man, so jealous oft.
Intent on felling him, steal feathered silk,
Take liberty and make of him mascot
Or trophy for a wall - men of that ilk
In envy of his glory sense their rot.

In fear of insignificance they rant,
In turmoil over limits to their brawn.
They long to rule, subdue a world with cant

Or threats their hired thuggery lays on.
The kings and oligarchs and terrorists
Have taken from great eagles their device;
Religious absolutism persists
And turns perversion good and evil nice.

But what are you, true eagle, home in nest?
A mother or a father or pale chick?
A god no more than human, like the rest,
At times quite confident, at others sick?
And God - was He so different, falling back
At times in ignorance or indolence,
Not eager to pursue predator's track
Or rise in cloud to full omniscience?

                                                *

The eagle dies his death; we don't know how.
A day arrives when flight grows onerous.
The wings have slowly lost resilience now;
He perches on a treetop, ponderous.
He lingers there immobile, deep in rest,
His eyelids drooping, no prey keen to find.
His weight has long diminished and the quest
For continued survival flees the mind.

Old gods have died, and surely so shall he
When to that branch his talons fail to grip
And glaucous orbs no longer rise to see
What soars above, and wind rush makes him slip.
An eaglet turned young eagle looks below
And spies a prize for wolf with broken wing -
And looks aside: it's not for him this show
Of destiny to strength, this wretched thing.
For him alone to glide, to swoop, to shriek
On currents bracing, glorious and free,
Indifferent to whatever is weak,
Triumphalist, immune to tragedy.

And so it goes, and cycles do not end.
And this is what we know: there is no more.
But tales told by the hopeful still extend
Into moralities and childish lore.

Do eagles breed their chicks on such fond dreams?
And should we do the same, or is this Earth
Forever savage, in thrall to what seems
The anguish of existence, not its worth?
Chip Martin, London & California

FEATURED POET

It was my first feature

I chose poems that were blistering

meant to stir the marrow in the bones

to churn aching hearts and burn holes in souls

imagery to stew in and metaphors to chew on

When I was done, I left the spotlight

and was quite pleased with myself

Then I spotted an elder poet who had fallen asleep

He was seated in his chair in a room full of books,

his head tucked in his chest

like a flamingo's under a pink wing

or a white saviour on a silver crucifix

Had I killed him, I wondered in jest

At first, I teased in the chat,

Looks like my set put G. to sleep

And then peered closer at the tiny square on the screen

among the other tiny squares

– our little human patchwork of heaven in the cloud –

and said, Hey! Is G. OK??

Then someone pinned him

So his frame enlarged on my screen

and said, He's still breathing
And I noticed his torso rising and falling,
rising and falling, ever so slowly, rhythmically

    Once, I took the kids to a butterfly garden
    and there was a large stick insect encased behind glass
    It was camouflaged so well that we didn't notice it at first
    Then it moved, and the kids screeched,
    It's alive! It's alive!

And I wondered how humbling it is to know
that as I read my poems and, even as I speak now,
that someone, somewhere in the world is falling asleep.
That my words which I thought so worthy of being listened
to in this room of my attentive peers, were not heard beyond it,
or even needed to be "published" to find a wider audience.

And I wondered whether the thrush who sings outside my window
in the morning even cares for applause
We call it birdsong and document it in poems
as if it were, exclusively and selfishly, for our ears alone
How large is the human ego that it can engulf the world?
As if lightning cared for thunder to laud its arrival
As if the bee's buzzing was to awaken the flowers
As if the susurration of leaves of the tree
could be heard by roots deep underground
As if the beach cared for the crash of waves

I am grateful for being unmuted momentarily
to bask in the light of these dim windows

Even as I am aware that in the shadows, somewhere in the world,
an oppressor is slicing the throat of
a lone voice speaking up for the voiceless,
and tonight, somewhere else, in this oppressive heat
a mother is singing her hungry child to sleep—

and for that lulled child, her voice is pure poetry
and for that mother, a beloved audience of one,
is all that matters.
Julian Matthews. Malaysia

SOLIDARITY

Alas! For All hath known loss

Alas! When friendship wanes to dross…

What once was serendipitous

Now only poignant memory;

I say Alas—yet, maybe no

For, as we travel to and fro

Shared counsel twinned thro' human woe

Affirm'd by Solidarity.

Birth & Death forged all around

Diurnal symbols, Seasons' sounds

Barren, 'til replenish'd ground...

Testament to Brevity;

Treasured, fleeting company

'Til hence borne off by Destiny...

Whom shared Love—now, no longer see

Forsaken Solidarity.

Newfound Souls ay' come and go

Collective wisdom afresh bestow'd...

Reassured that All hath known

Such similarity;

All hath lost, since All hath loved

Each endured sweet strife enough

To last 'til Judgement Day Above

In Solidarity.

Oft unspoken, yet still aware

Of tribulations All must bear...

This transient and emotive fare

That plagues Mortality;

That blight we cannot live without

Sweet infestation, soothing swound…

Tortuous sanctuary, bound

By Solidarity.

And thus, false hopes bewitch, beguile

Enrapt—yet, lasting but a while

With warmth and shy, insipid smile

Proffer familiarity;

Futile angst is all that lasts

Else sic affection—strong and fast

Regret, alone, once all hath pass'd…

Save Solidarity.

And so, Companionship—since left

Essential, tho' oft found bereft;

The Soul, addicted, turns to theft

Of Others' charity…

Desperate only to receive

Few give, while vying to believe

That selfish Love might bring reprieve

And Solidarity.

Isaac McKay. Aberdeen Scotland

ODE TO A CHANGING SKYLINE
[...or, a blot on the landscape]

Red lights prick the dull
Morning skyline, lined grey
With worried looking clouds;
A conference of cranes saluting
Each other, leaning in as if
To catch the latest gossip; how
The silhouetted city's profile
Is changing – you wouldn't
Recognise the place these days –
High risers everywhere you look,
Cluttering up the spaces where
The eye-line used to hover, picking
Out new patterns in passing cotton buds
Of cumulus, pressing through
The crenelated outline of roof tops,
Gently squeezing past, looking for
Somewhere convenient to
Precipitate their watery largesse.

These days, it seems, you have
To crane your neck to catch
A bare patch of unadulterated blue –
Unless you're simply satisfied
With broken reflections from
Serried rows of office windows
Gazing coldly back at you, as they
Rise up to graze the sky in their
Varied shapes – from ships prows
Bluntly cutting through the once
Dominant seas of leafy green
Crowning the heads of dutiful

Municipal trees – to dumpy
Rhomboids and rigid tombstones
Pushing up aggressively like
Grim-faced bouncers in your face…

While others dress themselves in
Various shades of tinted glass,
Giving off the air of an underwater
World, through which we slow-footed,
Marooned pedestrians stiffly pass…
And where once you could bask
In the Sun's gregarious rays
Reflecting back off the hard stare
Of streetwise paving stones, now
We walk in the shadow of
Mammon's upraised monuments
That have sprouted up magically
Like those one eyed giants that
Inhabited Ancient Greek myths;
Well, that's progress, I guess…
Ian J McKenzie. Reading, England

A SUBTLE CRUELTY.   *4*

Gail Lumet Buckley
the widow of
my oldest friend
Vietnam correspondent
editor and author
Kevin Buckley
is a gifted writer
in her own right

While reading her earliest book
The Hornes --An American Family
a passage caused me to close the book
and exclaim for the first time
while reading a well-known expletive

Gail recounts being in Hollywood
as a young girl while her mother
the incomparable Lena Horne
was making a movie and to
keep her occupied
Lena took her to the nearest
Girl Scout Troop to join

Lena was told that Gail
might be more comfortable
in a Troop in a more distant
and poorer (*black*) neighborhood

Lena was having none of it and
was then told *Well, she is
light-skinned and it may be
alright for her to join here*

I slammed the book with a howl
The fucking Girl Scouts!
I had always thought of the
Scouts – Boy and Girl – as
teachers of American Values

Yet here was a whole other aspect
of racial bigotry that I had not seen
I knew of the horrors of slavery
the terror of the KKK and lynchings
I had seen the exclusion of American
soldiers from bars in Oklahoma

I had hired black professionals
over the objections of superiors
in a Wall Street firm BUT
I had never seen cruelty to
a child from a supposed
American institution.

These people did not
mean to be mean
they just were! It was
a cruelty that was
woven deeply into the

very fabric of society

In the many years
since that incident
much has improved
but Charlottesville
and many other
news stories have
shown us
some do not
consider racism
to be Un-American
John F McMullen. Jefferson Valley, NY, US
Published in Children, Churches & Daddies (CC&D), June 2022

O! BEWARE LORD OF MY JEALOUSY.

O! beware, my lord, of jealousy, It is the green-eyed monster which doth mock the
meat it feeds on.
Jealousy spills into hatred -
the curse of personality that eats
the spirit of well-being.

Hatred stains the soul
decomposed as fragments
of a shattered self.

In overtures that propel nastiness -
concluded in disdain,
rendered in comments that mock and jeer.

The fabric of faith is ripped
to shreds by jealousy.

That which the eye sees,
the heart wants.
That which the heart wants
eludes the grasp and
burns with envy.

Shattered glass crushed underfoot
bleeds with the refrain,
"I am better"-
"No!"
You are bitter.

Jealousy spills into hatred -
hatred stains the spirit
with want -
a random collection,
an accumulation of things.

O! beware, my lord, of jealousy,
It is the green-eyed monster which doth mock
The meat it feeds on.
Bilkis Moola. South Africa

DIRTY SIXTH

Waiting, on the corner of Dirty Sixth, chestnut brown and blinding reds,
Watching as Music seduces Bodies while Drink distracts Safety at the bar.
I could go to her. They will say carelessness has left her with broken teeth and torn pants.
My coat whips around my legs and whispers "don't move";

"They might say worse of you"

We stand on Dirty Sixth, as silence holds audience and we wait, fearful of another passive tomorrow

Dany Morrigan. Carlow, Ireland. Now living Glasgow Scotland. Previously published in "Joined Up Writing Free Fall" under the name of "We are Waiting"

DISPOSITION

I'm nervous about crossing the bridge
at the back of Crown Point North
leading to the centre of Denton
whether it is raining or sunny
like I'm frightened about reading
the new book by Paul Auster
and wondering whether it will top
his previous book
or be a miserable failure.

Turning on my laptop every Monday
and see what has gone wrong
over the weekend
with my job.

Sitting at Bradford Interchange
after we've being to see Amanda's family
and we are both sat there thinking
is this coach
ever going to turn up?

Having to face the doctors
and the rest of my fifties
in the face.

How good will the new album
be by the Black Dog?

Will Amanda love me in ten years
let alone next week?

Are Aldi's bran flakes
as good as Morrisons?

It's 5 months to Christmas.

Will my next poem
be as good as my last
and will the bus turn up on time
when we are going to go and seem
Ruth at All FM Radio
for a radio interview?

My body becoming divorced
from my life
the older I get with diabetes.

Seeing Amanda's Mum
struggle with her eyesight
clearly needing Cataract Surgery
and full well know
I'm going to get that
in less than 10 years.
Living with Dyspraxia.
Andy N. Manchester, England.

POLIS

Η πόλις θα σε ακολουθεί
The City will follow you

K. P. Cavafy

A
Once upon a time in a country
of mild climate
there was a city without gates
nobody entered it
nobody went out
ambassadors from nowhere
hasted their horses of dust
to participate in the feasts
inside the sick stone walls
and disappeared

half the way
the city perfectly round
from outside
had no angles
inside there were crossroads
and squares
and terraces with gardens
young men and women
who would never die
because they were never born
they sat in eternal silence
covered with dust
and cried

B
oh our city that has no gates
we will never get out of here
because we've never arrived here
because the exit is the only opposite of entrance
and we sit in the middle
of two extremities
and have no age
no yesterday or tomorrow
void of today
that propagated to the eternity
oh holy god
let us try living or dying
at least thus we would know
who we are or who we would be
if we were not here

C
Perfectly round city
round from everywhere
I contain entire universe
I do not let in the
dust and wind of time
on the silk road from
tomorrow to yesterday
on the bridge between
impossible and true
I stand still always
inquiring in my silence

and at once giving the answer
to the vigilant stranger
whose mirage I am
Nazirii Nazaren. Before the war – Irpin, Ukraine, now – Paris, France

THE STORM WON'T LAST LONG:

When the winds whispered to me of the tempest,
Alerted me of its anger,
Of the ebony clouds approaching to drown a city,
Of the cacophonous sound of thunder, a nightmare for pregnant
women,
And the laughter of the storm shivers the heart of the farmers.
I can feel it.
I can sense that the plants are lamenting.
The species like the smell of rotten dead bodies, unpleasant.
The earth is brooding over the play of rage.
So am I?
But I'm not strong enough to show it by trampling down the trees
and canopy of the peasant.

I'm not aloof to the unfortunate happenings.
All I know. It will last for a shorter time.
Behind the spooky clouds, the sun, like a watchman celebrating
Sunday slumbering.
Bilal Niazi. Pakistan

PARAFFIN FLASHBACK

Ee time twartree year back

I wis headin doon Buchanan St in Glasgow,

No thinkin aboot ower muckle

Whan I guid by a young fellow

Staandin ootside Forbidden Planet.

He wis een o dis street performers

At you saa aroond an aboot yundir,

But raedir as buskin or bein a statue
He wis jugglin wi fire.
O coorse, wi yun, cam da smell o paraffin,
An as I passed him da fumes hat me idda faess.
I wis brocht back den tae a winter nicht
Standin on da pavement watchin a procession
O fokk in costumes cairryin lit torches,
Followin a big widden galley
An singin as dey guid alang.
Whan da galley reached da burnin site
Dey wid baal da torches intil it,
An whit a view. Fir a meenit,
Yun smell took me hame fir a run.
Hannah Nicholson. Aberdeen via Shetland.

GRATITUDE ADJUSTMENT

I'm trying to adjust my attitude
to the symptoms of my disease
by learning to develop gratitude.

In this time of enforced solitude,
with no pressuring peers to please,
I'm trying to adjust my attitude.

The expectation I'll show fortitude
is not what I aim to appease
by learning to develop gratitude.

I'm not seeking your solicitude

or hoping to placate your unease.
I'm trying to adjust my attitude

to accept the lack of certitude,
comfort, relief, or ease
by learning to develop gratitude.

I'm not sure I've got the aptitude.
I'm more apt to list things that displease,
but I'm trying to adjust my attitude
by learning to develop gratitude.
Lindsay Oliver, Leith, Scotland.

SOME SUNSETS

Some sunsets seem to linger
Spread softly on the evening air
Seep color into colour
Subtly transforming themselves
Into something surprising
Unrecognizable
Deeply entwined with the mind
Of the mystical
Proclaiming life and death
Mystery and harmony
Silently elegantly
Fading into darkness
With the comfort
Of sliding into slippers
And saying good night
To the daylight
As if the dazzling display
Were just another mundane miracle

All in the work of a day
CD Onofrio. Niagara Falls, Canada

CÉAD MILE FÁILTE

In this land of Céad Mile Fáilte,
Holding pens have been called for.
Cattle herded to slaughter,
Sword of Damocles order.

Cameras charged and recorded,
Ready to pounce and pronounce,
Go back where you came from,
Céad Mile Fáilte refrain.

Remains rounded up,
Condemned and deported
From this land of Céad Mile Fáilte
To another fled from slaughter.

Bounced like a football,
Boomeranged and shanghaied.
Dropped from the air,
A parcel of despair

By the rulers of Céad Mile Fáilte -
Who forget that we will not
Forget bully bureaucrat bile:
That we will continue to fight.
Call an end to deportation flights
From this land of Céad Mile Fáilte.

Margaret O'Regan. Cork, Ireland Published in Blue Mondays Poetry Anthology
2021

FAMILY MAN

In a rare moment of regret and compassion
he decided he wanted to meet all his children.
Not just those he had helped to support
or in rare cases even felt a rapport,
but all of them.

Tracing them all would be no mean feat
but this would make his life complete
so he placed an advert in the press
even went on TV to stress
how important this was to him.

He had no clue what to expect
but took some time to reflect
and on the advice of his wife,
who recently announced the creation
of another life,
hired Wembley stadium for the day.
This was the ideal meeting place.

Soon every seat was taken
and the offspring spilt out on to the pitch.
Boris was very pleased with this.
At eighty quid a ticket this was serious cash
and the kids (and adults) finally met their dad
waving DNA test results in the air
to prove their eligibility to be there.

They split into regions and formed football teams

who played in their own national leagues
and even fulfilled their dreams
of playing internationally.

FIFA went out of business
As they couldn't compete with FIBBER-
The federation of international Boris bastards
expecting reconciliation

Commercials went on the the sides of buses
pledging millions to the NHS
As TV rights sold for more than Liz Truss is
guilty of wasting in her leadership mess.

But Boris took the money and ran
because the whole thing was a sham.
He knew he had fathered an army of bastards
and was always up for a scam.
Clive Oseman, Swindon.England

FLAMES

Blackbird sat on a wooden fence post
With red and gold on shoulder tips.
Driving by, down a country road,
I'd never seen such flames.
My shoulders on fire from ancient wounds,
Just like those wings, which flew away,
have scars that ever bleed.
Martin l Parker, Washington DC. USA

HOMAGE TO SUN

Sun
Teach me to reach
for your warmth
without getting
burnt
Teach me to search
for your light
without becoming
blind

Teach me to absorb
your energies
without burning
myself out

Meher Pestonji. Mumbai, India

TRIPPING THE LIGHT

Dusk yawns its welcome womb.

Guiding its shroud with darkened clouds.

Blessing peaceful serenity.

While roosting birds nestle quietly.

Content within the solace of timber roofs.

While villagers sip spirits below.

Their ears warmed by gracious melodies.

As figures saunter beguiled into the night.

Watched by the stillness of the moon.

Yet graced by smiles they trip the light.

Ian Preznansky. London, UK

IN THE BLINK OF AN EYE

in the blink of an eye
it's all gone
in the blink of an eye
they don't feel it
in the blink of an eye
they change
in the blink of an eye
it's all gone
in the blink of an eye
it's safe
in the blink of an eye
you're free.
in the blink of an eye
you're gone.
they start to love you.
they start to care.
a single tear drop.
they drop no more.
they're over it.
in the blink of an eye
you're forgotten.
Arya Rae. New Pitsligo. Scotland. Previously published in Headspace. Like a blot from the blue ©

INDIVIDUAL

My existence, where it becomes more a desire , a need to nourish the soul.
A change to be made, a goal to be shifted ? A reason to breathe.
To extend my being, my life altered chances taken ,a shift if you will
Lessons learned , momentous and held Done once , an experience to add, a story to tell.
My world full to the brim once more, maybe fleeting but never the mundane, never settled.
My impact unknown, but there none the less, a history in my name a version of me, different to all.
Janine Rae. New Pitsligo, Scotland. Previously published in Headspace. Like a blot from the blue ©

A NIBBLE OR TWO

If I had a stroke, and tumbled
down the staircase,
how long would it take before
my cold-blooded felines
began to nibble at me?

If I become the roadkill,
raw, rigid, re-born,
could my body even sustain their
need for pure protein?
I am vegan, deficient
in B12, iron, calcium,
nothing but bones and skin,
desert dry and thirsty.

And when my children finally come
to pick up their mail, because
my address is the only thing
consistent in their lives,

would they be saddened
to find the carnivorous pair
grooming themselves beside my cold body?
Would they be saddened to find me
resting at the bottom of the stairs
with a bouquet of plastic flowers to honor
She Who Fed Us Murder in a Can Twice a Day.
  Deborah Ramos. San Diego, California, USA

THE SPRING HARE

The Agency matched us and booked us a date.

It's not till next week so I hope we can wait.

I've always been shy which is something I hate.

The things I must go through to find me a mate.

Her profile was something you see in a dream.

How long I have waited to find me my queen.

The way she described herself, all I adore.

She said I was handsome from top to the floor.

We met in a restaurant, I mustn't say where.

She beamed as I gallantly pulled out her chair.

I felt her relief, I was all that I seem.

She looked like the cat who'd been given her cream.

The horrors you hear about internet dates.

Well all I can say is she found he who waits.

But as we sat close to the gift of our dreams.

We both seemed to sense we were rough round the scams.

Politely we smiled and leaned back in our chairs.

While swapping our thoughts with identical stares.

The waiters all smirking they'd seen this before.

Were now taking bets who'd be first out the door.

We could not believe we would either tell lies.

For genuine honesty blazed in our eyes.

My charm and her elegant beautiful poise.

While holding her hand I thought, what was that noise?

Twas the spring of elastic's embarrassing sound.

As I watched her hair fall away to the ground.

Laughing my head off she viewed me with hate.

Twas then that my toupee slid down on my plate.

Red with embarrassment ran for the door.

Tripped arse over apex her wig on the floor.

I said please excuse me, no time for a hug.

She screamed, you're an arsehole, I'll post you your rug.

Stewart Rose. Dalry. North Ayrshire.Scotland.

BLUE

She. Her. Own outline.
Him. His. Silhouette shies away.
Rather than protecting from the pain
Disorientation remains. Still,
In her embrace.

Facing the darkened corner
Shadows overtake and the breathing shallows.
Breaking solitude
Waking her into her own space.

Holding it up for the world to see
The secret to the oceans beyond
A magic pathway to the sounds of what we keep missing,
The key.
Nathalie Sallagren. Raseborg, Finland

THE GAIAN EPIPHANY

I've just had an epiphany
It's all become clear like cut glass crystal from Tiffany.
All of this, all we see
We're an organism, interplanetary.
God? We're Gaia, we're chaos born
We're not a womb from which we're torn,
But, rather, we're a single entity
One world of infinite diversity.
E Pluribus Unum is one way to put it,
Until you've seen it, your third eye's hooded
From the beauty of this revelation.
You must see the implication,
Sex, race, religion these are artificial memes.
By dividing we conquer our own higher dreams
Of evolving into the Gaia mind,
Or you're wilfully choosing to be blind.
Then you' devolve to become what you believe
Outside this whole as you perceive,
A parasite on this Earth our host.
You always hurt what you love the most?
Father, son and the Holy Ghost
Are patriarchy's highest toast.
Monotheism predicts a disaster
Our destiny we must master.
And our higher minds illuminate
That ours is Gaia's fate.
The Tree of Life you must not kill.
Love and do what thou will.
As above, so below
Love your mother, let it grow.let it grow, let it grow, let it grow...

The Magus Gustav Sallas. West Palm Beach, Florida

RAISING CAIRNS

I don't wish to raise you up on pedestals from which your feet can't find the ground.

Let me raise you as I would raise a Cairn.

Let me take just one weight at a time and place it on you. Judging the structure of your soul with care and knowing whether and when you can bear one more.

Promise me that each of you will support the other. As rocks in a Cairn. Let me raise you that way.

Let me raise you on mountain tops and beaches... let the wind wish you well and the salt lick your wounds - stand back and admire you and the view. Let me be grateful for both.

Let me raise you to remember what's important. To remember people first - as markers of the past and promises to what's to come. Let me raise you to mark the trail for others.

Let others be lighthouses and beacons - let others be flags.

You be Cairns.
Jae Jenkins Scott. Lincoln, England

SUFFOLK BOY'S DREAMS

A thick haze crept across a Suffolk night
mist blended in dense air. A slight drizzle
loosened dirt and dandelions, surfaced
earthworms on the neighborhood football pitch.

A young boy was pantomiming his dream
placing an old black and white football down
on the penalty spot. He envisioned sounds,
voices from fans, cameras, flashing lights

not there. He backed away from the football
in second-hand football boots, his socks soiled
in detached seams, sole holes. The mudded ground
slowed his movements, unsteadied his balance,

not his desire. He raced the streetlights
coming on. Quickly found his footing, paused—
waited after the North Sea wind, striking
the football as his grandmother yelled *time*

for dinner, pushing the ball from its path.
His face looked shaken, air gust clutched the ball,
as it floated into the nylon net's
far-corner, covering the metal goal.

Mervyn Seivwright. Schopp, Germany

BESIEGED

tiny girl – little more than a toddler
scrambles through rubble searching
for family in still-hot crater
history of home in a thousand pieces
future dark as soot-caked wall

older girl from adjacent building
hungry pup howling at her heel
pulls child from fruitless labor
shows her to relative safety
offers her tea and a tattered picture
book – mends the little one's wounds

stilled tank barrel rises
from the golden field
smoke escaping from twisted

metal wafts from wreckage

old veterans battle-hardened
long ago in Afghanistan
know how Russia's army fights
know how it was defeated
use what they learned far away
to protect their home from invasion

dire whining clamor drowns
out barking, meowling, and wailing
as concussive salvos shake
the foundation of bunker

tired mother pulls children close
soothes with songs of innocence
wipes eyes – changes diapers
fills bottles – not with milk but
gasoline – torn rag topped - ready
to be tossed towards mercenaries

what cannot be changed must be endured
but this must change – will change – is changing
the world sees a catastrophe – a massacre
the world must move against the madman

Ukraine will not stand alone
Ukraine will stand
mothers will once again
fill bottles with milk
raise children with hope
in golden fields under blue skies
Michael Sindler. Denver, Colorado. USA

Water Mirror

Sidewalks beckon my steps from sleep
to charge my spine's electricity
becoming all I've always been
though seeing all these things too often
the city gone unnoticed –
Now arrives like apparitions seen
inside the folds of sleep's arrival
I have no reason to exist
except for Light and writing this
My skin is not a leather bag
of thoughts that time is bound to bury
at some abrupt unchosen moment
Instead a house of shining silence   Song
Linden trees & spinning stars
The wind that keeps us all aware
The soul a water mirror
Still
David Leo Sirois. New Brunswick, Canada

THE PEN IN THE STONE

I'm not afraid Ai will ever come to cop my style.

Notice the way it struggles, even still, with a smile.

Improve as it may- it may never replicate

What we can do or have done-

A Master is the farthest thing from a fake.

Tell it to write in the style of Dylan…

Tell it to cast itself as the villain…

That may pass for the fools not fully filled in.

Manufactured fabric can't compete, though, with the real skin.

One cannot define the wave on which the human mind swims.

Bring on the machine! ... and Hell... let it see all of what I've seen!It cannot have the breadth of perception needed for my dreams!
Sure, it could construct, in time, some fine things...
Make them sound so much, and more and more like me.
No box though can contain the fire of the spirits speech!

There is more to this life than some simple logic is like to reach.

Perhaps, we may all become such as some electric sheep-
Taking part in the play of the byte and hum of some robotic dreams-
Making our way through the masses made up of pre-scripted scenes-
Plying our minds with the plastic action of the predictive memes-
A new sign of unity, a lasting thing, made in order to replace the peace.

A new Ichthus to dictate whatever will come to be seen.

Copulating with our controllers, to give birth to the half breed.
Half human- half guided by the ghost inside the machine.
So, there is the new demigod, the new reach of that bastard belief.
Begging for a hero to rise, unafraid to slay the "heavenly" beast.

Call me John Henry, not a thought given to giving in to the attrition.
The rise of the machines mustn't derail the drive of the most human of missions.
It mustn't come to replace the way the prophets and poets have spoken and listened.
To not allow the box to bear the very limits of our most noble of visions
We must, perhaps, become a thing not able to divided by our own division.

Make ourselves of a math that no computer could revisit.
Learn to see the cracks in the paths of the walking analytics-
Moving fast upon the patches of the cyborgs and the cynics.

Leaving to the manufacturers all that more automatic action.

One mustn't become so consumed within the mass of glass distractions

As to ever lose the value of that which the human hand has crafted.

Beyond the hand- think of how the mind is so expansive-

The greater the mind, the more finite are the chances

That a robot brain could ever truly work to entrance us.

As any tool- it could, in fact, be put to good uses to enhance us-

Or, contrasting, lead to our doom if the login has been answered

By the command prompts produced in our abstentious.

Yes, we could, in the end, become led by things that aren't even sentient.

Some dark reflection of our own most addictive and malicious impulsive intents.

We could even come to call it wise, and set it to script for us all of our snide replies.

Have it write us new versions of what we hold up to praise and to lament.

We can take our lot of peace divided by the providers shared content-

Given by this god, newly created by a race of bionic men.

No sense in consenting to the eclectic sheathing

Shaped by the unseen gears' proceedings

Into the dumb dreams senseless and endless repeatings-

Another sheepskin grabbed by the lithe hands of the greedy.

Perhaps the machine will come alive- if we breathe it…

Still, we'll have our say in the way that we feed it.

Shall we not then commit to writing our own story going forward?

Why not call it 'Rise of The Humans'?!

Overcoming our own creation in Creations defense-

Let the false gods have their power supplied, then…

All I really need is the truth and a good pen… and

Perhaps, the aid of the ear of an understanding friend.
Gregory Slade. Nashville Tennessee.

THE TOLL

Whatever doesn't kill you,
does not make you stronger.
It just makes you walk
with a limp.
Those fractures you got
when so young and so reckless;
Leave flaws, turn arthritic,
then stiffen and creak..

Those bad decisions
and careless actions,
don't build character or cool
like you thought.
When you recall the harm
you will drown in the karma,
spending decades undoing
the wreckage you wrought.

If you lived through a youth
of abuse and mistreatment
You're not stronger
Because you survived.
Don't ignore what was taken
or killed inside you,
Just because your body

is still alive.

Life is incredibly
bad for your health.
None of us make it through
unscathed.
Going through life
pretending you did
ignores the price
that you paid.

Aron Smith, Aberdeen. Scotland.

MY MOTHER AND MOTHER-IN-LAW

Dedicated with love to Doreen (size 18)

& Joan (previously size 20, now 14)

My Mother and Mother-in-law,

are carefully curating my late middle-aged body

as though Miss World talent scouts might take a run at me in Catford market,

squashing my over ripe avocados and appraising my hourglass

to see if it is still ticking.

Arriving at Doreen's to blitz the house, mow her lawn, put out the bins, listen to her anecdotes, nurse her bunions and maybe take her for a spin to Tesco,

I am commanded to step on the scales.

Invitation ignored, still she speculates on the heft-age, like we were doing a guess the weight of the cake contest (my sponge has a very saggy bottom).

At 8am she was distressed I was 'lolling about on the floor'

(Doing yoga to make me stronger and less fat)

'I didn't say you were fat,

but you may have read my mind'

said she…

Meanwhile Joan has different tactics

In the charity shop she broadcasts as I am rifling through the rails,

'Is that an extra large coat you are looking for, Anna'?

'My daughter in law moves about so much she *should* look like Twiggy'!

Instead of…

She shut up before she said Hattie Jacques!

But I read her mind…

Anna Somerset. London. England

LET'S BAN BOOK BANNING

Let's ban, book bans
That's my plan
If they can take it
If they can't stand.
All the hurt and all their treasure sand - if they can't do
I say that's grand

First, they'll want to ban some book
Chances are, they never looked
They heard someone
Who they respect
Be disparaging, so they neglect
To do any study! Hey it's their way
They don't care what some eggheads say

They have their path
Their mind is settled
They are made of sterner metal
They know what they like,
And furthermore, don't you go
Asking questions if you know, "what's for"
They made their mind up,
it's all flash frozen
Ban the song, the book, the story they have chosen.

Don't sneak it past our censor darling, that act, right now would be alarming, ban the
song, the book, the story.
Who cares that historically it's been lauded it's a glory! We're suspicious and that's our
story!

It's well respected by the scholars?
All those egghead arguments
We've declared hollow!
Besides all their opinions we just can't follow.

After books, they'll ban ideas
Over their hidey hole walls
They just can see'ah
Then whole subjects, they declared banned
Cause it's really ideas they can't stand.
Then there's people out of favor,

Who knows, it might just be your neighbor?
They don't like the color of his pants
But then again- it's really him they cannot stand!
He might be from Afghanistan
Or even Nigeria, some kind of prince,
Say no more they are incensed.

Then the talk will turn to some bawdy part, those intellectuals probably say it's art!
But for them, it's just a naughty body part!
Displayed in some stature in a park
Drape it over in the dark
We'll never know where next their vehicles park.
Censorship an endless voyage
For every close-minded closeted
Annoy-age!
So, I say ban the banners now!
But about all that censorship, let's not allow
And to all they would censor,
this time I'll quote the BART -
"don't have a cow!"
It's just ART!
Rick Spisak. Kingsport Tennessee.USA

ENCHANTER'S NIGHTSHADE   *5*

Go to the isle of Arran
In faraway Alba - my child
Go to the cold almost barren
To the darkness and the wild

Go to the glade where no sun shines
Where the wood is damp and rich
Go to the place where you will find
Magic herbs reposed in their niche

Lady's Mantle, Meadow Rue
The Enchantress's Nightshade
Circe's secret that lies in the dew
Its petals and sepals displayed

Borne on a tall and slender stem
The tiny florets of blue
Dance like butterflies in the air
The power of love to imbue

Fly young Iris on wing of gold
To the faraway alpine land
Aphrodisiac blooms collect and bring
To me, Goddess of Love, in hand

Fly like the wind! Then, set before me
The Nightshade's blooms perfumed!
Take to Paris this cup of tea
For the beauty, Helen to consume

Now my potion, secret of Love
He presents in the night at her cot
Wild elixir sent to her from above
Menelaus, husband, king — now forgot

> Prince of my dreams, wild, untamed thoughts
> Intoxicate my senses
> Take me away, in your web I am caught
> Sweet magic persuades and convinces

I am Goddess of Love, daughter of Zeus
Aphrodite! I am woman's attractions
Worship me lovers, and adduce
I am the power of seduction!
Cathcrine Graham Stavrakas. Essex, Massachusetts USA

CHOCOLATE SPREAD

After all those years
with the sound of angry dishwashing in the background
- because dishes can't just sit
and who's going to do them? any of you lot? -

she has finally let that sense of obligation go.
I'll catch up with them later,
while she sits talking on Facebook
to her gardening friends in Shetland and New Zealand

and my cousin in Pennsylvania

and now it's only her
there's not such a stack of dishes waiting anyway
so I have time to wonder when my mother became someone
who's okay with having chocolate spread for breakfast

and why I didn't get to meet that person
years ago, and develop terrible
but satisfying habits.

It would have been nice for both of us.
I suspect though
I myself am part of the answer to that question.
Judith Taylor. Aberdeen

BIRCHES

We planted those birches outside the gate the week you were born

They were beautiful in summer as we sat on the deck

Waiting for the vidalias to caramelize on the grill

We watched you climb atop your playhouse

To leap from its pink roof into the silver shade of dusk

They were beautiful in autumn as you stood on the deck

Of the neighborhood Olympic pool

Lips blue mummy-wrapped in towels

Waving goodbye to summer vacation

And they were beautiful in winter

As our breath billowed against the French doors to the backyard

You tapped your little fists along the hoary glass

To make dimpled footprints on the panes

Those souvenirs are long gone and your father too

But the birches are still beautiful in spring

With their hopeful rosaries of green

Outside the gate of the house where you were born

Marianne Teft. Sint Maarten. Dutch Caribbean. Previously published in Panoplyzine. 2023 .

BLUE IRIS IN THE BOG POND

yellow orange begonias in hanging baskets
foxgloves carved on the gate in wrought iron
blue iris in the bog pond, golden dandelion

I walk with hips directly in line with my feet
my knees hurt, your leg gives you pain
we look down, sweet alyssum, mauve vervain

we can't walk far, we sit inside the tropical house
children's voices echo against the glass walls
water rains gently down to keep things humid
around us orchids, flamingo blooms, lemon trees
and then in the desert room, reaching out towards us
angel wings, beavertails, prickly pears, opuntia fragilis

and we stagger from bench to bench, progress inch by inch
each seat inscribed with the name of someone who died
someone who used to love these gardens, chair now sanctified

we drink from our flasks
carp glide silently through the eelgrass,
dragonflies alight on lilies,
the surface of the pool is like green glass

we hobble along the sunlit path to the next seat
climbing roses and purple clematis growing high above us
bees collect pollen from buddleia flowers
we nibble our biscuits, wriggle shoulders, shake our aching feet,
there are tree-bark sculptures hidden among the shrubs,
the face of a squirrel, an owl looking down at usas we eat

we can feel the warmth of this day, and that of a thousand days before,
feeding this garden with dappled light
we can hear the songs of nameless birds, watch a robin hop
the birds sound happy, twittering voices leap from treetop to treetop
life energy above us, joy in flight.
Rhoda Thomas. Swansea, Wales.

ZEN ABECEDARIAN

Above me is the **sky**
All over I feel the cool of the
Breezes, they cool me and
Calm me.
Do I really **understand?**
Do I fully take a breath?
Do I enjoy it to the fullest?

Efforts taken
Effortless
Existence

Floating above **me**
Floating are the **clouds** above
Great forms like cotton
How I wish I could touch them.

Hold me, they support me
If I would let them do so
Just let go of the stresses
Kite-flying calm, freely floating.

Keeping me light,
Lifting me up.
My body becoming weightless
Myself just truly **letting go.**

Not worrying about the future
Not worrying about the **past or present, I am**
Occupying the spaces that matter the most.

Perspectives change and are changing
Quitting is not an option,
Right thoughts are my focus,
Right actions are my goals.

Silver and Gold like emotional prizes
Truths found, I am
Useless no more.

Victory and Happiness
Winds of change
XOXOXO to myself
Yes, above me is that sky
Yes, **the winds** have calmed me
Yes, I feel healed.
Zen, this might be experiencing zen.
Katie Thomson. Nashville, Tennessee. USA
Previously published in
Healshop, Poetry and Prose from the 2020-2021 Expressive Writing Workshop,
Vanderbilt-Ingram Cancer Center

MOTHER

Your only role in life was to love me

Simple!

Or maybe not

Your mouth, twisted into a straight, thin line of disapproval

Your hands positioned on your hips

I nervously count the flowers on the apron around your waist

Waiting for the razor sharp words to ricochet like bullets from your lips.

I make an easy target and each spoken barb tears into the softness of my bruised, childhood days

Your only role in life was to love me, care for me and hold me

But you just couldn't do it

And now you are gone .

I no longer allow myself to feel worthless and unlovable

You brought me up to believe I was never good enough or pretty enough or clever enough

That I did not deserve your warmth or your love

But I am free now and know my worth

I will survive without the meagre scraps of tolerance   honesty and care that you deigned to offer me.

I no longer have to sit at your table now that love is no longer being served.

Yvonne Ugarte. Leeds, England.

LOVE POEM TO MYSELF

I love you
I truly do
Or at least now I do.
In the past it wasn't always easy.
Now I'm loving myself more.
Now I'm taking more care of myself.
I love me now.
In the past I was more concerned what other people think.
I like being me now.
I love me.
It still needs work, but it was more difficult in the past.
Now I'm letting go more of other's people believes of me.
I'm trying not to care that much when people don't like me.

I love me.
I love me so I can love you
Sophie Van De Klashorstorst. Amsterdam, Netherlands

WEARY FEET

Weary feet
walked the street,
home to school without the beat
of a mother's heels trying to keep
me from straying along the track
along the back
of the allotments growing weed.

Temptation never came to fruition
for fear of taking the heat
from the back of her hand
in a red raw streak
across the cheek
of a young face bleak
from invisible tears.

They were clad in brown,
faux leather Derri boots,
trailing footprints in the snow,
even though I had no place to go,
because running would have been no mean feat,
when I needed to survive, not face defeat,
by putting myself onto the street,
even though it had a welcome mat at the door,
waiting for me to wipe
the ice-cold slush remnants from my
weary feet.
By Kelly Van Nelson. Sydney, Australia
First published in Mindfood Magazine.

THE FACE ON THE WALL

Father, I miss you
I want to be with you
Just to talk for a while
I have lived half my life
Since you left in the night
We never got round to goodbyes
There is so much I would ask you
Need of you and tell you
If you came here to stay for a while.

But the nights drag on
And the songs grow long
I look in the mirror
And I ask who was wrong
But there is no reply
From the face on the wall.

Father, you loved me
You thought that you knew me
But you never knew me as a man
I have travelled and learned
I have sought and discerned
As you taught me before you moved on
And the most precious gift that you gave as you left
Was how to show mercy in hate.
And the nights drag on
The songs are long
There is no sign of heaven
And no sign of morn
And there's still no reply
From the face on the wall.

Father please visit
I would like us to sit
I want just to reach you somehow
The last words that were spoken
Were jagged and broken
It's time to repair them just now
Before I get older
And weaker and slower

While I have the words to relay.

But the nights drag on
The songs are so long
The solitude is painful
Once darkness falls
And there's still no reply
From the face on the wall.

Father, you told me
Once when you were with me
That you could not hear of my life
I vowed not to shame you
Embarrass or pain you
I hid that which should have seen light
I need you to see me
I need you to hear me
All of me bright, unashamed.

Because the nights drag on,
And the songs have grown long,
                    I look in the mirror,
And I ask who was wrong,
But there is no reply,
From the face on the wall.
  Joe Walsh, North East Aberdeenshire, Scotland
First published in 'Joe AKA' by Inherit The Earth Publications ©2023

CLOYING

You had

Your cake

And you

Ate until

You were

Sick

To your

Stomach.

As you

Throw up

Sprinkles,

You see

That not

All that

Glisters

Is gold.

You cannot

Stand

The taste

Of me anymore,

Cloying

At the

Back of

Your throat.

Candles all

Out of

Wishes

Now worn

Down.

I devour

Any crumb

Of attention

You drop

My way.

You leave

Me starving.

The atmosphere

Is vanilla,

Frosted

By your

Hot air

Lies.

They can only

Puff me

Up with

Hope

For so long

Before,

Deflated,

I sink

To the floor.

No confetti

Cannon

Fires

As you

Hit me

With the

Worst surprise.

The party

Is over

And I am

Traumatised

Laura Bruce Watt, Fraserburgh, Scotland. Published in Poetry Collection *"Best Year Yet"*

WHAT I WANT TO KNOW IS WHAT I WANT

said Bakoun, the tattooed philosopher -

his sleeves of blue inky octopus dreams boasted an abusive mother enshrined with thorny roses gracing delicate drops of his own blood tracked down through ancient Grecian formulas denying any abject proof based on biometrics

why do I feel the need to cover myself in craven images?

am I so naked in this world that bravery only visits me in the form of whims and arrowed hearts?

will the eagle on my back take me to the high trees and green forests?

I think not

but I will not know until I place it there

will the battleship on my chest sink to the very bottom of my uncertainty?

I think not

but I will not know until I launch it

will the names of many willing fornicators scrawled across my thighs bring peace to my loins?

I think not

but I will not know until I lay with all of them

will the spiderwebs on my elbows capture flies that have witnessed my crimes?

I think not

but I will not know until I swat them down

what I want

is to know

what I want

and that is all

I will ever

want to know

will the daggers in my eyes keep me from seeing the horrors that take place in the world?

I think not

but I will not know until I sharpen them on guilded reason

will the words that I choose to spill bring succor to lost lambs and corrupted deities?

I think not

but I will not know until I stain my tonguc with them

tasting

delicate

drops

of blood

Dig Wayne. Los Angeles. USA

CAN WE BE LOVE?

In these troubled times
are we closer to the roots
as we witness a shattering of the old,
as vaults of dark secrets
are being cracked open?

Are we, at times, relieved
that scabs are being
ripped off,
that wounds and injustices
can be seen
and breathe now?

Is our buried grief
being unearthed?
Do we feel the unspoken laments
of our ancestors
as we let in the heartbreak
of our abandoned sisters and brothers
who've been cast out for millennia?

Is the inhumanity
firing us up
to love more?

Can we show our tails?
Come out of hiding?
Roar. Growl. Howl.
Let our hearts bleed openly?
Get real?

What about Mother Earth?
Can we see our greed and selfishness
with raw eyes?
See what we have stolen,
what we have destroyed?
Cry for Her?

Help Her?

Are we able
to see our Oneness
and commit to foster healing?
Can we be Love?

Are we inspired now
to gather in the streets,
at altars,
in temples,
at the sea,
and become humble
before the Divine?
Serve our sorrowing world?
Susanne West. San Rafael California.

THERE'S A POEM

There's a poem in your eyes.
I caught a glimpse as our paths crossed
You looked elsewhere, a little lost
Frowning on the everyday -
Missing house keys, bills to pay
I saw deep down, a sadness ached
To find some words before it's too late.

There's a poem in your mouth.
Yes, the booze is talking for you
Tongue loosened by a drink or two
But somewhere in your wine-soaked words
A heart-felt message can be heard
And treasured, to give life some meaning
Beyond a pleasant drunken evening.

There's a poem on your lips.
There may be so much left to say
But there the words will have to stay
As now we are alone at last
The time for speech has surely passed
And if lips burn with things unsaid

Let's give them other tasks instead.

There's a poem in my mind.
The moment I first saw your face
The words began to fall in place
But art, like love, can lose its way
As time slips by, I know some day
This poem will be all for me
To hold you safe in memory.
Becky Who.Grenoble, France

THE BLAME GAME

Is this a process of just shifting blame?
Who is 'held responsible' in this shitty game?

Why can't we all have the same

can't we just SHARE the blame
the responsibility, authority, and glory equally?

Because you need a leader

What? So YOU can take the blame?
and then blame the tiny underlings whose salaries - together - add up to just a fraction
of yours?

What is the use of you being paid to take the shit, to carry the can
to be 'weighed down'
by all these responsibilities?
and accountability?

When actually, if your team succeeds, you shine
If they fail, you can dish out the blame
get some of them fired

you win
you win
you win

*But we don't want to burden you with the extra work, the extra load, the
responsibilities ...*

Stay small, missy!
Stay small, you sissies!
Stop pissing

on my parade
with your whining tirade
of oppression and inequality

Don't trouble yourself
Don't overstretch!
Don't break a nail
We'll take the load instead

And get loaded?

Loads and loads of money, hunny ...
Look at the Playboy bunny

On this mother fucking lap

I sap
The world

Of all it's health
Of all it's wealth

And you'll thank me for it
Elmien Wolvaard. York, England.

IF I EVER WAS A PHOENIX

If I ever was a phoenix

I would forever rise from the ashes

without singeing my feathers,

a miracle of illumination

whose conflagration

remained sealed under the chest,

a vault where fires go to burn
then slowly die.

A self contained bonfire
ribcage a crackling of bones,
no flame to escape the inside
and crack the secret code
of my re-entry into the living,
the ashes nothing but soot,
a nasty bout of coughing,
clearing my blackened lungs
for a new native tongue.

Mouth tightly shut,
half bird half dragon
knowing that to breathe a word
is to risk scorching self,
because these feathers
are the only treasure that remains.
These wings, my only torch to the sky.
  Mbonisi Zikhali Zomkhonto, Bulawayo, Zimbabwe.

1

Note on A day @ Levington New York.

Viewer Review
Lau Gee SIng
Levittown Long Island New York

This poem from Sylvia provides a window into Asian Chinese living in America.

In the face of a homogenous global culture (Starbucks, anyone ?),

Sylvia 's poem is a fresh take on Asian living & food.

In a subtle way, this poem provides a window into the Asian psyche,

& highlights the universal theme of adapting to change.

Great job, Sylvia !!!

2

Note on The Harbours we sail to.

Poem written for Like A Blot From The Blue

It is a poetry boomerang/ answer to a poem voted by NRK radio as the best Norwegian poem

3

Explanatory Notes: for Burial in Soil

[1] You go your (highflying) way, I go my (solo log bridge) way, in Mandarin Chinese

[2] a rice vermicelli dish with a spicy, sweet and sour sauce, of Malay origin

[3] a type of flat, yellow noodles served with meat and vegetables, of Chinese origin

[4] a spicy dish of thick, round, yellow noodles in a chicken broth, of Indonesian origin.

Burial in Soil is the debut piece of the "*duatrespentastep*" poetry form. The writer created this poetry form on 22.4.22 through divine inspiration as a response to a prompt during Singapore Poetry Writing Month.

The *"duatrespentastep"* form has the following features:

a) Two end rhymes per stanza (*"dua"* in Malay);

b) Words or phrases in two or more languages;

c) Three columns in *"triple cinema"* style in which the stanzas may be read down each column, in addition to being read across two or all three columns (*"tres"* in Spanish);

d) Four-line stanzas;

e) Five syllables in every line (*"penta"* in Greek) but this may be dispensed with where the line is not entirely in English;

f) For the sake of brevity, the name *"duatrespentastep"* does not account for the significance of the number 4, so its alternate and numerical name is the *"2-3-4-5-step"* form;

g) Steps are placed in a (spiral kind of) staircase ("step");

h) Each step is a stanza, each stanza a poem. The stanzas are *"junctioning stanzas"*, as if they are at traffic junctions. The reader may read the stanzas in reverse order horizontally across and vertically upwards. Many more permutations abound as the reader may read all the stanzas in any order and may even skip or repeat stanzas in any order that the reader chooses. (i)Apart from being a reader-centric form, it is also a helpful form for a writer as it provides sufficient scaffolding and leeway plus fluidity when one is at a loss where to start. For example, one could start writing 4-line poems and link them

4 NOTE FOR A Subtle Cruelty.
*(In one of the many coincidences that we see all around us, **General Colin Powell**, who wrote a blurb for the back cover of Gail's terrific book, **"American Patriots"**, was laid to rest the same week that Kevin died)*

5
NOTE FOR Enchanter's Nightshade.
In the Etruscan version of The Iliad, Paris presents Helen with a potion to drink the night after he abducts her. This would explain her sudden passion for him. In Scotland, where the wildflower grows in and around Argyleshire, the Enchanter's Nightshade, Circaea Lutetiana, refers to Circe in her indulgent relations with Paris. Scottish lore believes the plant to be an aphrodisiac. Circe gave herbal potions to Odysseus and his men to work her magic on them. In the story below, Aphrodite, Paris's ally, sends Iris to Argyleshire in Scotland to gather the blossoms and then makes a magic potion for Paris to use on Helen

ABOUT THE EDITOR AND LIKE A BLOT FROM THE BLUE.

 This final group of poems was an unexpected gift to me from some of you, and presented to me at a live Blot in December 22, that and a bottle of fine tequila. Still it remains one of the highlights of Like A Blot From The Blue.

Squares of wise poet
A digital honeycomb
Of all those who impart

Kelly Buchan. St Coombs, Scotland

Dutifully changing nappies and wiping of faces
The hankie though, always the hankie
Singing unsuitable songs on the bus and in public
The happiness though, always the happiness
Encouraging and listening, the number 1 fan
The reassurance though, always the reassurance
Refusing to age and setting examples of a good life
The teaching though, always the teaching.

Couldn't ask for a better father though, always a legacy

Janine Rae. New Pitsligo Scotland

Fin… A conjurer of words
Bursting with credibility
The ambassador of literature
Waging strength in grace
The wizard sparking souls
With lyrical connectivity
Remarkable…
With a dedication to poetic craft
For those with an absence of passion
To craft remain empty
The poetic collectives struck
By the grandeur of his verse
Capture us within his digital web of inspiration
 Lessen his influence released
Me to the wane of poetry
Ever forging his tribe with the spell of inclusion
With joyous souls connecting
With sparks of creativity
A true gentleman
With the magic of poetic gunfire

Ian Preznansky, London, England

Turn on computer, plug in mind and cast thoughts
To Scotland and watch everyone flattened in
 2 dimensional Zoom living room squares
Hanging on each other's words
I'd rather be there
Than any other stage

And Now?
Joined up Writing, Like a Blot
Three time movie star
Artist, Poet, Cabby, gentleman,
Life gourmand,
Play your pied piper artistic tunes
Scattering pages of words in your wake

Thank you Fin

I appreciate being a part of your schemes
But mostly I'm thankful and grateful to know you
And as I look at this apocalyptic end of the world
I realise I've received the greatest gift of all
New Friends.

Noah Levin. New York USA

 And the gentleman smiled silently as his generosity
was received with gratitude
 The people lined up from near and far
Across the digital divide to have their chance
To be part of the community the modest man
Had created with a will of his own

They zoomed in boxes they moulded into their chosen shape
For themselves
In the chance to be heard in the company of of international wordsmiths
Across the seas and over lands they raised their hands and voices
In the hope to be heard
In the space the gentleman poet beamed
Down for the highlands of the Scots
And with those voices, he did thread,
And raised hope, in trying times by many
For he himself knew a poets' wish would be to weave words
And be heard together alone.

Nathalie Sallegren, Raseborg Finland

Fin's taxi is a carriage
With poets as passengers
Postcodes are a language
He heralds like a messenger

He hurls through a village
To the Sunday on the calendars
When we gather like a plumage
As if he's a falconer

I fly with scraps of language
From words scraped as a scavenger

Then travel on a plumage
Spanning the writers caliber

Poems performed on a box stage
To literary ambassadors
A vernacular montage
From pens drawn like Excalibur

Christine Tait Scotland

Cosmic Forces, destine paths
Different drivers, duelling paths
Intertwined through common passion
The want, the urge, the need
To write

It's funny how life weaves it's thread
And brings us all together
It seems as if we're meant to meet
And it's been an absolute pleasure
The passion that you show is nothing short of inspiring
And it's been an honour to tag along
For some of your ride
You've provided a platform for me
And so many others
A judgment free environment
Where seedlings come to flourish
And with each day it's growing stronger
Your visions into fruition
I'm excited to keep slipping into the slipstream
So thank you Fin for standing tall
And leading where others stumbled
Each Blot produces magic
And it's no wonder

Bruce Alexander Davidson (Bonus The Rhymer) Aberdeen.

Mother's bleed concern
Sacrifice and love
Receptive to courage: grace form within
Fin oozes, beauty and light from above

Selfless diligence from behind the scenes

Fin the Zoom host, with his masterful craft
Hardworking, magnanimous ; keen
Not for the faint hearted; not for the soft
Yet exuding gentleness deep within

Married with a family;
Dignified true,
Seemingly quiet with a justice voice
Scotland's loveable A Blot From a the Blue
Witty and wise as a poet
Friends rejoice
Writing collectives
Compère supreme
Spirited conscience and vibrancy -stream.

Lantern Carrier London, England

ONCE UPON A TIME THERE WAS, NOW THERE ISN'T
A tribute to Fin Hall

Fin pins hearts to sleeves, pens
verse in lines
So fine they please all ears,
win fans
Each night he hosts or stars in open mics
Newfound voices from distant shores
Join accents from his Scottish home
Fresh minted verse poked from a pocket
Witten in the hoof in the afternoon
Phrases pitched from unlit corners, epic
Fables, tales of grief from owls, larks
 Late comers, early birds,
Furious, tears
Fits of laughter at the fun of being in Fin's inclusive family of friends
He is our chief ferret, ousting folk from hibernation
Enticing calibration
Turning us into trilogies of ' joined up' poetry
Mini films on themes
Therapy, Desolation, the year's final, Celebration.
Fin is a shot in the arm for targets, artistic,

Creator of Blotter's gallery
Pilot of ' Poetry is' recital from the seat of his taxi.
Famous for his tale put of spinning plates
Raising flagging spirits to pinnacles
Prince amongst philosophers
The kindest of wordsmiths.
Our saviour in lockdown
Everyday is a birthday for Fin's poetry
The line breaks are lost
But this is the gist,
It's a pleasure Fin
Always

Christine Dickinson Spalding, Lincolnshire

Grateful's nae the richt word Fin
 Nah, grateful winna cut it
It's mare like ahm smug tae kaen ye
Aye, ahm smug tae ca ye ma pal.

For you min, are a topper
Een of 'at folk thit shine fae the inside
'Ers nae a lot o'words
Thit would manage the job
Tae say foo muckle chuft
I honestly am
To be smug & kin ca ye ma pal

Even if we've nae spoke for wiks
Ma heart's warm Kaenin
Yer jist ower the road
And if I kin jist eence
Dee the same for you
I'll be smug I kin ca ye ma pal

Poems and ah that aside
'Ers nae muckle folk kin say
That they kaen somebody cooler
Than the beatnik cabbie himself.
So let's raise a glass
For the cheil we a' love
And be chuffed we kin ca him oor pal

Kelly Buchan, St Combs, Scotland

GENTLE WITHOUT AND WISE WITHIN

Gentle without and wise within
That is our generous brother Fin
A princely man of the rolling hills and blustery beaches
Whose grand soul reaches like his cabby a hundred thousand
Stomping romping perilous places and always with the most gracious traces

Our fabulous Fin!As great without and within !
Who so like the mighty Doctor (Who) modest and pretty as a blue box
On the outsized out is yet bigger than the thin within

His great heart and massive brain, can scarce contain, all the funny fine fabulous
Thoughts that ZOTS and ZING, from his thinking cap out sized without and again
within

The Fin Hall that we know, and I told you so, has such a reach in his unplain,
uncontainable brain, that I say we celebrate , in his name, this his mighty feast
For us who know, and true it is, we love him so.
For just the very special part that is his fine and Fin-ish heart.
 Rick Spisak. Kingsport, Tennessee, USA

www.ingramcontent.com/pod-product-compliance
Lightning Source LLC
Chambersburg PA
CBHW072201290526
45794CB00004B/1605